What People Are Saying about Jennifer James's *Thinking in the Future Tense*

"If the hallmarks of a masterpiece are simplicity, clarity, and insight, then Jennifer James has presented us with a work of such magnitude. By showing us how to "think in the future tense" she addresses the central issue in meeting the challenges of the future while providing us with the guidelines for successful navigation of the sea changes around us. I recommend this book highly for all who seek to become more aware and productive in the years to come."
 —Charles Garfield, Ph.D.
 Author, *Second to None* and *Peak Performers*

"For those of us in the change management business who are eager to make an impact beyond the current moment, *Thinking in the Future Tense* is required reading. Dr. James presents a rich blend of stories, tools, and intellectual challenges, making this book worth reading more than once."
 —Martin H. Borell
 Partner, Change Management,
 Andersen Consulting

"*Thinking in the Future Tense* is timely, illuminating, and hopeful. This book shows how to get the jump on change. The chapter "Recognizing the Future" itself is a complete course in product analysis and development. Every business should look at itself this way."
 —Lawrence H. Merk
 Director, University of Idaho
 Center of Business Development & Research

"*Thinking in the Future Tense* isn't just a formula for surviving in a bewildering, changing world; it is a blueprint for thriving in it."
 —Lee Lathrop
 Manager, The Boeing Company

"Jennifer James shines a brilliant beacon across the horizon of time and brightly illuminates that sometimes frightening but most often fascinating mystery called the future. *Thinking in the Future Tense* is an exhilarating and empowering experience."

> —Jim Kouzes
> Coauthor, *The Leadership Challenge*
> and *Credibility*

"Jennifer James helps give context to the future. Her insightful work can be an invaluable tool to those seeking to move forward and embrace change and explore tomorrow!"

> —Paul J. Greeley, Jr.
> President, American Chamber of Commerce
> Executives

"*Thinking in the Future Tense* provides a visionary plan for business leadership in the next century. Those who execute it will have the competitive advantage."

> —L. Alan Witt
> Barnett Banks, Inc.

"As humans, managers, decision makers, and family members, we are being pulled in a dozen different directions. Jennifer James challenges our thinking and equips us with fascinating insights into our past, present, and most importantly, our future. Read this book. Twice."

> —Glen G. J. Wong
> Executive Vice President,
> Rogers Cable TV Limited

"Outstanding mind stretching, humorous. Margaret Mead has been reincarnated, and she cares about American business."

> —Alene Moris
> Executive Outplacement

"Jennifer James's new book shows how the mind can reach further and deeper and faster."

> —Dale Chihuly
> International artist, Chihuly Studio

"Thinking in the Future Tense is a truly intriguing and positive reflection of the oft-stated 'the past is prologue,' which, logically translated, says, 'You haven't seen anything yet.'"
—W. Hunter Simpson
Retired CEO, Physio-Control Corporation

"Insanely enlightening! These things need to be said."
—Larry Diamond
CEO, Diamond Productions

"Thinking in the Future Tense will energize and move you to grow and develop. Jennifer James's ideals will increase the speed of your development and provide you with tools to accelerate the transformation of your organization. It has certainly done that for me."
—Baron Stewart
IBM

"Thinking in the Future Tense contains the missing ingredients in the formula for tomorrow's survival skills."
—Abe Kessol
Director, Spectra Physics Scanning
Systems, Inc.

"Thinking in the Future Tense is an important addition to the evolving body of literature that is preparing us for the kind of thought processes we need to successfully cope. At a time when we are deluged with change of every kind—in demographics, technology, the workplace, economics, and society—combined with a tidal wave of information, books like this will help us keep our personal focus and ground us on shared values."
—F. A. Blethen
Chairman and Publisher,
Seattle Times Company

"Thinking in the Future Tense is inspiring, energizing, and hope-filled. Jennifer James understands the dynamics of radical cultural change. She makes complex information immediately accessible and presents the future through understanding the past in an engaging, vivid style."
—M. Maureen Maxfield
Vice President,
Sisters of Charity Health Care Systems

"Jennifer James once again offers us her superb intelligence, clear provocative writing style, and extraordinary creativity. She thinks in the future tense as a matter of course and shows us how to do the same. This book is essential for those who feel anxious and overwhelmed by changes around them. For those who feel prepared for the coming decades, she will stretch and challenge them with original perspective and hard questions."
—Jackie Farley
President, CenterPoint in Aspen, Inc.

"Jennifer James takes a refreshing new view of leadership. Understanding her perspective of our past, present, and future is necessary for any agent of change to be effective."
—Todd Clist
Executive Vice President,
Marriott Corp.

"The richness of *Thinking in the Future Tense* lies in James's understanding of what makes people tick."
—Tom H. Timmons
Vice President, Mobil Oil ExCom

"Just the chapter on the power of myths and symbols will be worth your time with this book. James's insights always have the ring of truth."
—Jeff Smith
The Frugal Gourmet

"Jennifer James is a lead scout in the arena of breaking mental models. *Thinking in the Future Tense* lays out the topography for each of the eight skills of building shared understanding and getting smarter with data. It is a treasure map to competitive advantage, an important addition to organizational learning, and a must for the new leaders."
—Charlotte Roberts
Author of *The Fifth Discipline Field Book*

Thinking in the Future Tense

LEADERSHIP SKILLS FOR A NEW AGE

Jennifer James

SIMON & SCHUSTER

To Ted

SIMON & SCHUSTER
Rockefeller Center
1230 Avenue of the Americas
New York, NY 10020

SIMON & SCHUSTER and colophon are registered trademarks
of Simon & Schuster Inc.

Designed by Irving Perkins Associates

Manufactured in the United States of America

1   3   5   7   9   10   8   6   4   2

Library of Congress Cataloging-in-Publication Data is available.

ISBN 0-684-81098-0

Contents

INTRODUCTION   13
    Star Trek Technology   17
    Smart Work   19
    Interdependence   21
    Understanding Who We Are   22
    All You Need Is a New Mind   23

SKILL 1:
SEEING WITH NEW EYES   27
    Perspective and Memory   31
    Distortions of Perspective   33
    Perspective Skills   38

SKILL 2:
RECOGNIZING THE FUTURE   50
    Driving Forces   53
    Predicting Change   56
    The Net   60
    Extension of Almost Everything   62
    The Characteristics of Entrepreneurial Minds   68
    Pattern Skills   70

SKILL 3:
HARNESSING THE POWER OF MYTHS AND SYMBOLS   74
    Symbols   78
    Myths, Symbols, and Business   79
    Noticing the Changes   83
    Myths and Symbols in the Global Village   86
    Myth Switches   89
    Myth and Symbol Skills   91

SKILL 4:

SPEEDING UP YOUR RESPONSE TIME   104
   The Processes of Change   106
   Testing Your Flexibility   108
   Styles of Change   111
   Dysfunctional Change   122
   Surprise Changes   124
   Making the Transition   126

SKILL 5:

UNDERSTANDING THE PAST TO KNOW THE FUTURE   128
   A Time of Illusion   131
   Lodge Cultures   135
   Corporate Cultures   139
   Leadership in a New Age   143
   Five Stages to Recovery   147
   Looking Ahead   152

SKILL 6:

DOING MORE WITH MORE OR LESS   153
   Energy and Security at Work   156
   Creating Energy and Security   160
   Keeping Your Life in Balance   170

SKILL 7:

MASTERING NEW FORMS OF INTELLIGENCE   179
   Understanding Who Is Smart   181
   Putting It All Together   188
   Thinking Skills   190
   Barriers to Thinking   196
   Future Skills   201

SKILL 8:

PROFITING FROM DIVERSITY   207
   A Multicultural Workforce   211
   Race and Ethnicity Myths   214
   Sex, Gender, and Image   217
   Diversity as a Process   219
   The Next Minority   224

CONTENTS

EPILOGUE   228

NOTES   234

BIBLIOGRAPHY   237

ACKNOWLEDGMENTS   241

INDEX   243

Introduction

I HAD JUST COMPLETED A five-week trek in Nepal. It had been a lifelong dream to climb in the Himalayas, and after coming down from fourteen thousand feet, I was serene but weary, not yet ready to reenter the Western world. I decided to spend a week in Malaysia before heading home.

In the ancient city of Malacca, rich in the sights, sounds, and smells of the past, I strolled the waterfront and wondered what the years ahead might bring. Questions that had been on my mind from Seattle to Nepal kept repeating themselves. What did it really mean to "think in the future tense"—a phrase I had used in hundreds of lectures and seminars around the world?[1] What sort of person would feel confident and accomplished one hundred, two hundred, or three hundred years from today? What could I tell people who cornered me after lectures and confided their fears of becoming unsuccessful or obsolete?

In the distance, I could see a church, an elegant stone structure I recognized as Anglican, dating back to the eighteenth century. It was striking for its material: flintstone, an English import rarely found in this part of the world. My mother's family grave site is behind just such a flintstone church on the southern coast of England. I walked to the entrance and opened the massive front door, hung on cast-iron hinges. The sound of my footsteps reverberated on the stone floors and walls as I walked up the center aisle. I was alone.

Until the last century the privileged were buried within these churches. Even in death there was a pecking order. Nuns were buried in basement crypts; priests, bishops, and people of wealth or rank were laid to rest in elaborate caskets along the walls or beneath slabs of stone in the aisles of the church. The nearer the altar, the more prominent the deceased. The center aisle was prime after-life real estate.

My eye followed a beam of dusty sunlight to a massive bronze plate over a grave near my feet. There in the gloom was a bold inscription—an entreaty:

Tell Me the News

I was taken aback by this unexpected command from the past. I knelt down to read the rest of the inscription on the bronze plate, tracing the smaller letters with my fingers.

My father was an Armenian trader, born in Rome.
My mother was born of Greek and Persian parents. I was born in Istanbul.

A thrill ran through me, and I read on. The man buried in this grave, Jacob Shamier, had gone out into the world of international trade at age sixteen, following in his father's footsteps. The epitaph revealed the details of his life. It was filled with the excitement of travel, of wanderlust, of discovery. Jacob Shamier died in 1774 at age twenty-nine, but his profound love of life and his passion for the future were apparently undiluted up to the moment of his death. The inscription ended with this singular plea:

Stand on my grave and tell me the news of the world.

So I did. I told him we had walked on the moon. I told him that we could talk to China by sending our voices through space. I told him about organ transplants and that many people lived past the age of one hundred.

I knew that beneath my feet was a visionary, a man who had embraced the future without fear. Here was someone who would succeed as easily in the twenty-first century as in the eighteenth. How ironic that the role model I was seeking for the future had come to me from the past.

Unlike Jacob Shamier, many people view the future with fear and dread rather than excitement and anticipation. The world is changing too fast for them. The future seems so unknowable and unpredictable. We are alienated from the present and ambivalent about the future. I call it the "cultural blues." We are afraid we are falling behind. We are worried about our society. We lack a framework for interpreting what is happening.

Thinking in the Future Tense was written to provide that missing framework, to help you analyze and organize events into a coherent picture of the future that will work for you and your organization. It is meant to be an exploration, a catalyst for your own insights, and a way to restore the vision so critical to successful leadership.

Understanding the nature of change is harder now because we cannot see the signs and signals that were once so obvious. Getting off a horse to step into a car was a pretty clear indicator that the age of mechanized transportation had arrived. Now change seems invisible, hidden in transparent pulses in the air. The appeal of a retreat to the past is not surprising. But it's too late to go back. We know too much. The new road will stretch out ahead of us regardless of our ambivalence.

Nowhere is that ambivalence greater than in the workplace. The "rightsizing" and social changes of the 1990s have turned many ordinary people into cynics and pessimists about the future. They have watched traditional career paths disappear. They have been laid off, or seen colleagues laid off and worry that they could be next. They wonder if they will be among the survivors or the victims of what seems to be nothing short of an economic revolution.

I have heard their voices firsthand. I am an urban cultural anthropologist with a special interest in adaptive strategies—how people survive in times of change. I lecture, conduct seminars, and consult with leaders of corporations and other organizations that are struggling to adapt to the new realities. When I talk with workers about how things are going in their companies, they tell me their managers often don't know what they are doing and won't listen to what the workforce has to say. When I talk with the managers, they admit to confusion but tell me they must follow ambivalent orders from executives. When I talk to the executives, they will sometimes admit to anxiety, not knowing what to do with conflicting goals.

We are all confused and ambivalent, trying to get our bearings in an age of such rapid change. We are experiencing an epic shift in the way we think and feel about ourselves and our jobs, about the way we live, and about the future itself. Leadership in such an environment requires courage, character, and a broader perspective.

When I ask teachers, "What are you doing to help our children develop the skills to handle this shift and cross safely into the next century?" they tell me, "We're waiting for the administrators to die!" They don't mean it literally, but they do not believe that people with vested interests in the systems of the past will be able to make the necessary gut-level and mind-level decisions fast enough to accommodate change. Administrators tell me the same thing. They wish they could fire teachers. There are already more computer-literate first graders than there are computer-literate first grade teachers. Can *you* beat a six-year-old at Nintendo?

The profound changes we are facing today would normally take two or three generations to be assimilated. We are trying to make the stretch in a decade. No wonder the result is anxiety and even chaos. We face a depth and breadth of change unparalleled since the Industrial

Revolution. The old values and institutions are breaking up, and we are unsure what will replace them.

Imagine this chaos as a five-thousand-piece puzzle that has just been dumped on your desk. What would be your first step in putting it together? Most of us would look for the outside edges and, if it was a square or a rectangle, search for the corners to create a frame. Then we would sort out the pieces by color, and the major images would begin to emerge. The change puzzle does have corners and a frame that you can piece together. The corners are: revolutionary technology, intense economic shifts, disorienting demographic patterns, and disruptive cultural transformations.

STAR TREK TECHNOLOGY

The technological shift is now familiar. We have entered the "cyber" age, a new culture of systems and connections. We have become cyborgs (cybernetic organisms), half-man, half-machine hybrids whose physical tolerances and skills extend far beyond previous human limitations. New technology always creates more human connections as it destroys old ones. In truth, we have been cyborgs ever since the first wooden leg was fitted onto a human body. Later, the patient in an iron lung was a cyborg. Now we have a dizzying array of cyborgs—humans connected to everything from hearing aids to pacemakers—and even part-time cyborgs (kidney patients on dialysis machines, airline pilots and the planes they fly).

Many of our children are highly accomplished cyborgs. The machine they are hooked up to is the computer. Young children don't read instructions; they make the intuitive connection, grab the keypad or joystick of the new machine, and take off. They feel their way through the moves of the game while we sit on the floor trying to understand instructions that tell you how to turn the power on but not how to play. You have to call a seven-year-old to find out how to get to the next level.

Chips and imagination are creating smart offices, smart houses, smart cars, smart telephones. We are being forced to use computers or lose access to libraries (the card files are gone), messages (voice mail), correspondence (electronic mail), gas pumps (automatic pay at the pump), and banks (automatic cash machines). The learning curve is straight up, but the payoff, as with all new technology, will take time.

The media marketers have categorized us according to our "technic" skills: *enthusiasts, hopefuls, faithfuls, old-liners, independents, and surfers.* Those who are less agile at navigating the information highway may have to pay penalties. Some utility companies, for example, now charge a fee for the diehards who want to talk to a person instead of a machine. A bank may charge extra for visiting a teller instead of using the automated version.

Technology already exists that will enable us to open our front doors by employing a voiceprint or a fingerprint: "Hi, this is Lee. I'm home. Open up." Our cars will unlock and start when we ask them to—unless we slur our words. Windshields will turn into transparent navigation screens, displaying the best routes to take and warning of trouble spots ahead. Eventually our cars will drive themselves while we read and sip lattes. A driver-free, fail-safe system is already being tested on Germany's autobahns.

Our cellular telephones or car radios will be useless to thieves when they operate only in response to our voiceprints: "Please stop, I don't know you." Computers will triple our writing speed when they operate by voice-activated technology. Electronic eyeglasses will create perfect day and night vision. Our bodies may eventually be reconstructed by "total prosthesis," the replacement of all body parts except the brain. Rollerbladers will have to share sidewalk space with "springwalkers" that move us along at speeds up to twenty-five miles per hour. We will also have access to what Motorola's CEO, Daniel Noble, once called "electronic nirvana." "Cyber-sex," or virtual reality eroticism, is already available.

Computer technology has dramatically changed our work habits. We hold international video team meetings and make video sales without leaving the office. We "pitch" clients via cellular telephone during drive time. Niche marketing is gaining a new meaning: finding the available spot in a client's overloaded twenty-four-hour day. There will be few assistants in our future offices. The computer will be our receptionist and secretary, handling telephone calls, messages, scheduling, word processing, research assignments, and more. Are you on board?

SMART WORK

The economic changes that swirl all around us are important to understand because they will dictate what skills will be in demand during the next century. Minds will be preferred over muscles. It has been estimated that 80 percent of the jobs available in the United States within twenty years will be cerebral and only 20 percent manual, the exact opposite of the ratio in 1900. A quadriplegic with good technical and communications skills is becoming a more valuable worker than an able-bodied man without those skills. We have upset the process of natural selection, by which hereditary traits that prove more adaptive than others eventually dominate. We are now evolving consciously, adapting our own bodies and minds to the necessities of survival. We must, in a manner of speaking, will into being new traits that once might have taken a million years to evolve.

Where does that leave our workforce? A large gap is developing between those who have high-level communications skills and access to electronic knowledge and those who do not. We are redefining not just work skills but the character and personality that are compatible with these skills. In effect, a new class system is developing and all of us are being confronted with unsettling changes in how we make a living—and how we live our lives.

Never before in history have we had an economic shift of this depth and magnitude. We moved very slowly from hunter-gatherer (ten million years) to agriculture (eight thousand years) to urban industry (two hundred years). But now, in what seems an instant, we are in a global service world speeding toward a bioeconomy that combines gene manipulation with electronics.

Vast numbers of people will not make it over this economic abyss. We are likely to see the largest accumulation of skill-disenfranchised people in history. But more is at stake than jobs lost. There is an absolute connection between the speed of this change in work, economic status, and mental health and violence. One of the first sociologists, Emile Durkheim, reported that high levels of drug abuse, domestic violence, child abuse, homicide, and suicide accompanied the shift from an agricultural economy to an industrial economy in England and France in the 1800s.[2] He also observed that people lost their old survival beliefs and felt alienated, a state he called "anomie." We call it burnout. It can lead to depression, exhaustion, and paranoia.

Today, we are experiencing the same loss of control and yearning for a simpler time as the nineteenth-century farmers who had to give up their land and move into the cities to survive. Suddenly, everything was unfamiliar—the work schedules, the sounds and smells, even their sense of time. They felt deep nostalgia for what they had lost, coupled with an urge to resist the new. Our reactions are similar, but the challenges are more difficult. The changes we confront are much more complex.

We must find ways to build new careers and new communities, much as other economic shifts in history have required, but we must do it faster and with greater sophistication. We must multiply our ways of perceiving—and then understanding—completely new economic realities. We might as well be pioneers in covered wagons, given the risk, the lack of guidance, and the spirit of adventure it will take to cross so much unexplored territory.

INTERDEPENDENCE

We are also surrounded by dramatic demographic changes. We have been told who is entering the workforce in increasing and eventually dominant numbers (women and former minorities). We know about the population increase of Hispanics (twice that of any other large American racial or ethnic group) and the historic shift in immigration to our country (away from the traditional European base to an Asian, Indian, and Middle Eastern flow). We have not been told how these factors will upend American culture and change our work, our politics, our religions, and our communities.

The onset of these new populations, as well as the mobility that has always characterized American society, has changed entire school systems, neighborhoods, and communities. In only a few years I have witnessed in my Seattle neighborhood a shift from Jewish merchants and fabulous bakeries, to African Americans and fabulous barbecue, to Vietnamese and fabulous spring rolls. Entire blocks of stores seem to put up new marquees overnight.

Demographic changes are difficult to accommodate because they require a basic shift in perceptions, values, and myths. Our combination of Native Americans and immigrants of every racial and ethnic background is unusually complex. It is, to paraphrase author James Baldwin, our greatest strength and our greatest weakness. It is our strength because of the passion, energy, creativity, and innovation that come from such a rich cultural pool.

It will give America the edge in invention and scholarship. We will continue to stack up Nobel Prizes. It is our weakness because a multiracial and multiethnic society is fraught with misunderstandings. People rub up against each other, triggering old territorial instincts, trying to hold on to traditional privileges. The result often is prejudice, violence, and the fraying of national hopes. Marshall McLuhan warned us in the 1960s that extending our reach would leave our nerve endings tingling. He believed that implosion and interdependence would be far more disorienting for modern man than explosion and independence had been for tribal man.[3]

UNDERSTANDING WHO WE ARE

With these demographic changes inevitably come cultural changes that we must confront and accommodate. Culture provides the organizing principles that all societies must possess. Culture is the "story" of who we think we are. But cultural beliefs also separate, through superficial differences, groups that reasonably should be united. Culture is at once the means by which societies try to solve their problems and the chief cause of their conflicts. America, for example, continues to struggle with ethnocentrism, the belief that your nation or group is superior. It may be the last of the mythical barriers to fall. In the future, there will be no "chosen people" or "children of the sun." There will be just us.

Anthropologists use social data and models from the past to provide a frame or a context for the future. The details of millions of years of history and hundreds of societies reveal patterns. When you understand these patterns, it becomes easier to predict cultural change. But because it is so deeply rooted in the patterns of the past, culture is often the last system to adapt. Vestiges of old beliefs hang on long after the technological, economic, and demographic systems have changed.

Our nine-month school year is left over from a once-dominant agricultural economy; our corporate hierarchy is not too dissimilar from the leadership structure of a monarchy, a church, or a Freemason lodge. Players struggle fiercely on the football field as if the fight were over real territory. We are more afraid of abuse at the hands of unknown members of other "tribes" than we are of the greater dangers that lurk within our own families or social groups. The old metaphors are powerful.

Yet cultures can, and do, change, and those who fail to understand that run the risk of eventual embarrassment—even obsolescence. Executives and politicians who behaved as if women would never earn equal status or as if homosexuals would never gain political power now must wonder if their careers suffered as a result. How must it feel to glimpse an old film clip of angry whites harassing an African-American child trying to enter a school—and suddenly see your face among them? Either you have to retreat into denial that it happened, rationalizing that you were just keeping in step with your culture, or accept that what you believed and what you did was wrong.

ALL YOU NEED IS A NEW MIND

Today, we all stand in a vortex of technological, economic, demographic, and cultural change. Are we to deny it, resist it, or accept the fact that we, too, must change? Our brains must adapt to our changing environment. I believe that our current assignment is evolutionary, nothing less than the remaking of man and woman into a more civilized form than our ancestors. We must do it, not within an extended family in a forest or on a vast savanna, but within what is becoming the human family in a global village.

We cannot go backward; we cannot stand still. This is a personal journey and we must *will* the direction.

There is no waiting for some evolutionary process of adaptation, because evolution as a biological process has no goal beyond reproduction and survival. But you can teach your mind to adapt to change, just as our bodies adapted to change through biological evolution. We must teach our children to increase their intelligence, to cooperate, to think in new ways. It is a tough assignment, but one that we must make a commitment to if we are to prosper in the years ahead.

The key is the ability to "think in the future tense." You need to understand how the currents of technological change will affect your life and your work, how economic changes will affect your business and its place in the global market, how demographic and cultural changes will alter your self-perception, your perception of others and of human society as a whole. In short, you need to know what the future will look like.

These are the skills you will need:

1. Perspective
2. Pattern recognition
3. Cultural knowledge
4. Flexibility
5. Vision
6. Energy
7. Intelligence
8. Global values

These eight skills are presented and described in the chapters that follow. They are the basic building blocks for understanding and adapting to change, essentials for anyone in a leadership role. Companies will continue to downsize, merge, or disappear. Knowledge workers will be asked to do more complex and subtle tasks. Business relationships will require more emotional intelligence. Executives will have to sort through confusion and mixed signals to make strategic decisions. Anyone who cannot adjust to the many new demands the future brings will be left behind.

This is a book about welcoming the future. It is about openness, reality, and reason. It is about expanding our access to wisdom, the understanding of what is true or right, of who we are and what we believe in. It is the nature of America to give each of us the freedom to be a sage. Once societies turned to kings, shamans, priests, and oracles for wisdom. People had a "calling" to be wise. Now each of us is called.

Seeing with New Eyes

"The real act of discovery consists not in finding new lands but in seeing with new eyes."

—MARCEL PROUST

IMAGINE YOURSELF ON THE roof of a building. A spaceship is descending toward you, the white, glowing saucer of science fiction. As the ship hovers in the air, a stairway is lowered to your feet. An ethereal arm beckons you into the craft. What do you do? Are you ready to enter the spaceship and meet the extraterrestrials? How curious are you? Do you want to know what they look like? They might need your product or services. Are you going to wait and see what happens to others who accept the invitation while you are still trying to decide? Or are you going to close your eyes and wish they would go away?

What if I posed these questions to a group of ten-year-olds? How do you think they would react? Even though they have been warned about strangers, I suspect that most would climb into the spaceship. What are the differences between you and ten-year-olds? Most people would answer "Experience." But have you actually had "experience" with an extraterrestrial? In fact, we tend to generalize our beliefs from past experiences. Your response to "aliens" would probably depend on preconceived beliefs about our universe and who inhabits it. What did your parents tell you about "new groups" that moved to your town?

We face the same dilemma when we think about the future. We cannot "experience" it until it becomes the present. We have to keep our mind and our eyes open. That is why the core skill for understanding the future is the willingness to see it—and to see it in perspective. Perspective enables us to think clearly. It is essential to sorting out the positives and negatives of an issue or a situation. It allows us to perceive how the pieces or parts relate to each other and to the whole. It enables us to accurately interpret change and adapt to it. It lets us weave new possibilities. A clear perspective is the linchpin in any process of change.

A closed mind narrows our view of reality, making change difficult. Trying to make sense of an event or a problem, we fall back on what is familiar. When we cannot put change in perspective, we are predisposed to reject any new information that conflicts with the familiar. We are fearful of the future because we do not know how to explore uncertainty and unpredictability.

Our perspective is shaped by everything from childhood experiences and old habits to race and gender. It invariably influences our reaction to change. When change speeds up and becomes more complex, as it has in the 1990s, the situation only worsens. We may lose our perspective altogether when there is too much information, too much complexity. We find it difficult to extract knowledge from raw information, to synthesize, or to strategize.

Losing perspective can make us crazy. The body will automatically react if it senses danger, but the mind may freeze. We hear words and we fail to comprehend them. We read a report and remember nothing. Some new high-tech machine appears at the office and we won't learn how it works. We have difficulty seeing what seems obvious to others. We fail to notice key events and we make avoidable mistakes. We lose our common sense. We feel blindsided. We feel like victims. But it is the loss of perspective—our inability to understand the past, comprehend the present, and envision the future—that makes us so vulnerable.

When the leaders of a company or an organization lose perspective, the results can be serious and long-lasting. IBM is an obvious example, but there are many more, from the automakers of the 1960s and 1970s to the timber workers of the 1980s and the American Medical Association (AMA) of the 1990s.

IBM never saw the implications for the future posed by Microsoft DOS because the company operated in a self-sealing culture that dealt with hardware, not software, and shut out "soft" information.

When I was working with Simpson Timber and Boise Cascade in the 1980s the workers told me they were unwilling to give up timber work as their way of life. They were not interested in being "nerds." Many believed there were enough trees for their lifetime, if not their children's. They thought the environmental movement was misguided and would pass as the hippies had passed.

The AMA complained that it was not invited to the table when the Clinton administration was developing its health-care plan. But the organization is a perfect example of a professional brotherhood that by its very nature is resistant to change. It could not read the writing on the wall in time to come up with its own proposals for reforming the health-care system. The competitive advantage rests with organizations or individuals who are not only aware of current trends but are able to adapt to and lead them.

But how can we lead when most of us have the feeling of overload in our brains? Do you sometimes walk across a room and forget why you are there? Do you ever have trouble spelling familiar words? Have you noticed people coming down the hall and you know you know them but have no idea who they are? Don't worry! There is nothing wrong with your brain. It's just that you are using it very differently than your ancestors did. Your short-term memory neurons are receiving data at four hundred times the rate of a Renaissance-era man. Imagine yourself a farmer one hundred years ago, riding around your land for a day. What data would you absorb, compared with driving to work now for half an hour, listening to the radio?

It would be amazing if your brain *didn't* feel overloaded. The average person's short-term memory can hold only five to seven bits of data at any one moment. If you put more items in, others fall out. The older you are, the more you have crammed into those memory circuits. Twenty-five-year-olds can remember things because they still have empty space. Some of us take our children to the supermarket in the hope they will remember why we are there.

But don't despair. Memory is rapidly becoming a far less important function. Gone are the days when we sat in animal skins around campfires, when the person who could name the medicinal plants or recite the oral history of the tribe was vital to the culture's well-being. Now we have computers—electronic memories, if you will. Already, surgeons wear headsets that retrieve information from their clinical data bank during operations. Rescue for the rest of us is on the way. I call it a "sidebrain," and somebody is making one right now. A big step past the Newton, Marco, or Envoy, it will clip on your belt like a pager and be voice-activated. It will answer your questions about spelling, math, scheduling, navigation, and other data. It will have a recognition beam, so that when someone is walking toward you, you can ask, "Do I know that person?" It will answer, in a whisper, "Yes, you do," and quickly tell you who that person is. As this book went to press, Parrot S.A. of Paris, France, debuted with a voice-driven handheld organizer/scheduler called Parrot.

Right now, we are all caught in the trough between increased demands on our brains and the arrival of the technology that promises at least a measure of relief. So while you wait, relax, keep your sense of humor—and write everything down.

PERSPECTIVE AND MEMORY

Our perspective on a behavior or event depends heavily on what we store in our memory about it. But memory, like perspective itself, can be very selective. We remember that which is satisfying or seems important to our survival. We especially remember anything that has to do with sensing danger or avoiding conflict. Personal stories stay in our memories because they engage our emotions. We forget that which seems to have no special meaning or relevance to us.

Memory provides a context for our perceptions. The environment in which we experience new information has a strong influence on our actions and reactions to that information. Here are some familiar examples:

- The power context: "I'd better concentrate now because this is my supervisor talking to me."
- The internal context: "How afraid or anxious am I about this situation?"
- The cultural context: "What have I been taught to think this is?"
- The self-interest context: "How can I get what's best for me?"
- The situation context: "Where did I first meet this person?"

If we lack a frame of reference—if there is no familiar memory or personal experience that we can draw on as we try to process new information—then our ability to compose an accurate picture of reality is limited. Without, for example, a frame of reference such as "tree," it is difficult to remember "pine" or "maple." Try remembering miscellaneous, unrelated objects that you glimpsed on a table and the limits become obvious. When our short-term memory is in overload, the challenge is even more difficult.

The memory likes a familiar context, the one that generated the thought in the first place. Walk back across the room to where an idea originated and it will probably pop back into your consciousness. Those brilliant ideas you had while swimming or having a drink, which you cannot remember when you are dry or sober, will come back if you return to the water or have another drink. Context can be everything. When we are especially comfortable with the context, we do better at remembering. That is why we remember things we agree with more easily than things with which we disagree.

Intense emotions will generate vivid contexts. You are likely to remember the most minute details of a life-threatening accident. Athletes remember the plays of a long-ago game because of the adrenaline rush that accompanied them. When you are cut off from your feelings it is far more difficult to make mental connections or accurately assess events. Your sense of self affects memory. A criticism in an evaluation by your employer might be remembered, while a compliment is not.

We remember far more in a rich, stimulating environment than in an impoverished or static one. The artists Monet and Gauguin sought environments that would expand their perception. Marketers who travel in other countries find that their minds retain far more detail in international negotiations than in local ones. They also pick up more new product ideas.

If our perspective is influenced by what is stored in our memory, so too is our memory influenced by the degree to which we can see things in perspective. Perspective enhances memory because it gives our brains the resilience and flexibility needed to stretch into the future. Remember the comic book hero Plastic Man. He could change shape to solve problems. With perspective, we can be alert to distortion and we can change the shape of our memories and our minds.

DISTORTIONS OF PERSPECTIVE

When the world speeds up or we feel personally threatened, we can easily lose perspective. Our distortions of reality actually protect us and give us a chance to catch up. We take refuge in denial until we gain confidence that we will survive the threat. Marshall McLuhan understood the importance of such defenses:

> Were we to accept fully and directly every shock to our various structures of awareness, we would soon be nervous wrecks, doing double-takes and pressing panic buttons every minute. The "censor" protects our central system of values, as it does our physical nervous system by simply cooling off the onset of experience a great deal. For many people, this cooling system brings on a life-long state of psychic rigor mortis, or of somnambulism, particularly observable in periods of new technology.[1]

Too often, we see only what we are prepared to see. When our ability to appreciate reality—particularly someone else's reality—is thus limited, our perspective is distorted. Studies of eyewitness testimony and jury decision making reveal how easy it is to perceive different realities if the manipulation of information neatly fits with what we already believe. The contrast between white and black perception of the 1995 verdict in the O. J. Simpson murder trial is a classic example. IBM's first negotiation with Microsoft is the classic business example of misperception of the future of computer software.

Robert Bly, the poet and mythologist of the men's movement, tells a story about farmers who would often find the skeletons of small birds in the lofts of their abandoned barns. The birds that flew in through open doors had become trapped when the doors were closed. They would attempt to get out by flying up into the rafters, not down to the floor to use the obvious openings beneath the barn doors. Memory and instinct make it very difficult to change traditional responses to a closed door.

Self-righteousness

One philosopher said that you can be right or you can be happy. I would propose this variation: You can be right or you can know what is really happening. Self-righteousness or smugness always distorts our perspective. By far the greatest proportion of people who are unaware, even psychologically sick, are those who feel entirely satisfied with their actions and thoughts. If you don't feel some tugs at your conscience, you are probably disconnected from reality.

Health insurance executives were so sure in the early 1990s that they provided a real and essential service that they did not see the consumers' loss of faith in insurance bureaucracies. The inflated executive salaries and hierarchical administrative structures alienated health-care professionals and customers alike. HMOs, for their part, did not see the value-added services that could be delivered more efficiently outside their own organizations.

When a culture begins to create a change in perspective, the shock always makes some of its members move to the extreme. That is why times of rapid change produce higher executive salaries regardless of company profits. Executives who believe they deserve and have earned multimillion-dollar salaries see no conflict in "lean and mean" when it affects line workers receiving minimum wage. It is just too hard to come to terms with new ideas if they affect your own sense of self. It produces cognitive dissonance. Rapid change also generates political extremists and single-issue voters. Thus, an antiabortion extremist murders a theoretical murderer—a physician—and feels justified. An Israeli extremist dehumanizes Arabs, kills them while they pray in a mosque, and becomes what he most fears, an executioner of innocent men and boys.

Age

Somewhere around age forty-five, many adults begin to cling to the past and react to any symbol of future change as a threat. Computers are a good example. Some otherwise intelligent adults still have an irrational fear of computers, which they view as alien, cold, threatening, impossible to operate. Sounds like cars in the 1930s. By contrast, children—with their wide-open perspectives—eagerly embrace computers. They learn to love this amazing technology in the same way their grandparents might have learned to love the automobile. They become adept at an early age.

Children are natural visionaries. Adults often shut down their intuitive responses because they feel clumsy and unsure. They buy their children or grandchildren Legos and Lincoln Logs, instead of computer design games, in the hope of demonstrating their superior skills at something. And yet, for both children and adults, the future—as symbolized by the computer—is the same. Only their perspectives are different. If adults could recapture the natural openness of children, they would be far less fearful of the future and far better equipped to cope with it. But age piles up negative experiences as well as positive, and that can limit trust in one's own mind or surroundings.

Gender

Gender-related concerns powerfully influence perspective. Fears over homosexuality, for example, prevent many men and women from seeing reality and accepting the existence of different sexual and familial lifestyles. At least we now joke about it in ways that were once taboo; homosexuality is one of many subjects now being desensitized by late-night comedians.

Women in health care is another example. I consult with many major hospitals and health-maintenance systems. Across the country there is a growing demand for women physicians in almost all medical specialties, including urology. (The exception is neurosurgery. When it comes to the brain, we still prefer a man.) Yet, some health-care systems are slow to hire and promote women physicians in specialty areas. Their bias is perhaps unintentional, but they can expect to steadily lose patients to facilities that have more women doctors on staff.

What is it about women doctors that patients like? The current preference of almost all women for a female gynecologist makes sense, but male patients also believe that women physicians will treat them with more respect and communicate more openly with them. This is a gender trend that will fade as all physicians increase their skills at communicating with patients.

Men in construction trades a decade ago used to complain to me that the presence of women took all the fun out of the easy banter of an all-male crew. Now many work side by side with women and tell me that they have learned to treat all their colleagues with respect and that the workplace is safer because of it. They can still find enough humor in the absurdities of life without making sexual slurs.

Class

Class systems like those in Great Britain, India, Kuwait, or South Africa restrict people's perception of reality, as does any human pecking order based on birth, race, color, gender, religion, or ethnic origin. Like tribal loyalties, they create an inability to work or live together easily in the larger community. When people share the same culture or species—or are of the same class—new perspectives are rare. It is like being in a sterile environment. There is little motivation for expanding awareness. Too often we see only what we are prepared to see—or what we want to protect from change.

When I am asked to consult, as an anthropologist, on the problems of an international merger, I shy away if the negotiations are between British and American companies. When they try to make a deal, there is usually an assumption on the part of the Americans that it will be easy because "We know the Brits. The British are like Americans." But the British are not like us. Their class system, while fraying at the edges, is still largely intact. It strongly influences their manner of doing business, which is characterized by nuances of acceptance and rejection that most Americans overlook in their eagerness to believe the British are so similar to them. The result is misunderstandings, unmet expectations, and, frequently, failure.

Even animals get caught up in class issues. Americans who are sensitive to the environment have eagerly supported the campaign for dolphin-free tuna. But one wonders about their perspective. While it is laudable to worry about dolphins being trapped in the nets of tuna fishermen, why doesn't anyone care about the tuna? Some tuna species are more endangered than dolphins. Perhaps it is that dolphins, as intelligent mammals, have been personalized as cute and lovable Flipper, while wiseguy Charlie the Tuna was never good enough for Starkist.

Electronic Media as a Distortion

Marshall McLuhan believed that the electronic media would eventually take over our ability to think independently, thus distorting reality. We would become glowing blue couch potatoes. The media is the message, and that would seem to be the case when managers and trainers use television images or computer icons as gimmicks to get our attention. Coffee cups, caps, and T-shirts are handed out like brand labels to remind us whom we work for, and many conferences are more entertainment than substance.

In fact, television fills us with so much of the experience of an event that we do not feel impelled to engage our imagination. Even if we were so inclined, there is always a commercial to break our emotional connection with what is on the screen. Add to that the remote control or keyboard, which allows constant stimulation with little effort. We give up our ability to concentrate, to synthesize. But we love it! We are like the blind-and-deaf pinball wizard in the rock opera *Tommy*. He liked the vibrations of the pinball machine. We like the fast-moving connections on the screen.

Television and computers are addictive because the need to use our senses is as insistent as breathing. We like to keep our neurons firing; random stimulation is pleasurable and modern work may be disconnected and tedious. Techies leave their computer screens on, decorated with flying-toaster screen savers, because there is a sensory thrill in a moving picture. As children, we used to stare at the black-and-white contrast test patterns on television screens, waiting for something to happen. Now we can make it happen, endlessly.

PERSPECTIVE SKILLS

An awareness of potential distortions of our perspective is essentially an awareness of the filters we all carry that distort reality and thus influence our reactions to change. Knowing your own limits is an important first step in keeping perspective. But there are also other steps you can take and attitudes of mind you can assume that will help you "roll with the punches" that come with rapid change. They are perspective skills and they are useful to anyone in a leadership role. They can help you build a better product or devise a new service. You can increase the efficiency of a production line or improve employee training. You can learn to predict the outcome of a trend and position yourself or your organization to take advantage of it. You can also better understand what is happening in your home or your society and decide what you want to do about it.

The Ability to Relax

Tension shuts down the mind and heart. When you are stressed from an unexpected or unwelcome event, you not only don't feel altruistic, you want to hurt someone. That's what happens in traffic. On a day when you feel fine, enjoy your work, know you're competent, and got enough sleep, you can drive the freeway and be in control. If someone tries to cut you off, you don't lose your perspective. You slow down, let him merge, and imagine he is rushing to the bedside of a sick child. Then you congratulate yourself for being such a good person.

But on a day when you are worried, had too little sleep, and wonder if you have the ability to handle your job, you hit the road already out of control. If people try to cut you off, you hate them. You hang on their bumper, make obscene gestures, or honk your horn. If the other driver is as stressed as you are, you may be courting disaster.

Relax! Many of the greatest leaders and geniuses (Edison, Truman, Einstein, Dali, Churchill) took naps regularly to clear their minds. That's what those reclining car seats, toilet stalls, and executive couches are really for. The ability to keep your body and mind in balance is essential to keeping your perspective clear.

A Sense of Humor

Humor lets you say and think things that otherwise would not be allowed. Humor lets you introduce an idea and then flip it in an unexpected way. Humor will keep your perspective tuned and get you through almost anything. If you cannot laugh at the absurdities surrounding you, you have a problem. That's why comedy is being made part of human relations programs in many workplaces.

When death jokes about your profession multiply, it's time to notice. When humor strays into previously taboo areas, like Richard Pryor's jokes about white women and Elaine Boosler's about men, there is change in the wind. Female jokes about men that are just as sexist as men's jokes about women are signals that the sex-role-change process is intensifying. "Why is it that women don't make good carpenters?" *"Because, all their life they have been told* [fingers held four inches apart] *this is eight inches."* "Why are men smarter than women?" *"Because women don't have a penis to keep their brains in."* Humor jolts our preconceptions and our perspective.

Insight and Intuition

Insight is "mental vision," one of the ways in which the mind escapes the limits of the obvious or the familiar. You are looking at things one way and suddenly you get an internal signal to look at them in a new way. People often laugh when they make this kind of discovery. "Aha! Why didn't I think of that before?" Inspiration is a valuable commodity. Managers and others with lengthy experience in a business or profession sometimes have trouble with this. They are so knowledgeable about the way some things "should" be done that they cannot envision doing it any other way.

Intuition is a combination of insight and imagination that was once attributed to spiritual communication. Mathematicians call it "fuzzy logic," drawing conclusions from vague or subjective input. The mind becomes aware without the direct intervention of reasoning. Once you can imagine something you can begin the process of creating it. Executives use intuition to make many product, investment, and hiring decisions, even if they deny it. Success in business may depend on an accurate gut.

Knowledge of Your Personal History

We know things only in terms of ourselves, but we resist self-analysis. Psychologist Sheldon Kopp warned clients to plow the fields of their past if they wanted to be able to plant their own crops.[2] Business consultant Peter Senge agreed: "Structures of which we are unaware hold us prisoner. Once we can see them and name them they no longer have the same hold on us. This is as true for the organization as it is for the individual."[3] Leaders gain perspective by figuring out who they are and what works for them, and then doing the same with their organizations.

Here is an example, taken from my own life, of how the process can work. When I was a high school student in my first jobs, I found it difficult to deal with male supervisors. Something in me deeply resisted doing what they told me to do. I knew something was wrong. But I did not know that childhood experiences had "wired" my memory to respond this way. When I became an assistant professor, the pattern continued. With men in positions of authority, I either didn't listen to them or passively circumvented their wishes. I enjoyed professional success, but there was never straightforward communication between the dean and me; in fact, I avoided him.

Fifteen years later I went to work for my first radio station and my program became number one in the market. I gave my new boss the same treatment. When he asked me to announce something on the air, I would agree but somehow never get around to doing it. The program was a big success, but I was uncomfortable, and after two years I decided to leave. On my last day, something unexpected happened. My boss called to me as I was heading out the door. Deep regret and frustration showed on his face. Only at that moment did I realize how much he had wanted me to stay. I decided that there was something seriously wrong with my ability to perceive.

I thought back to my father's domination, his harsh attempts to control me as a child. I realized that my lingering but deep-seated resentment of his behavior was influencing my attitude toward men in authority roles. I enrolled in an assertiveness-training course that taught women how to negotiate fairly with men without being afraid. I learned to be direct. I learned to respect the individual on the other side of the transaction. My perspective on male authority figures and my respect for male negotiation styles underwent a complete shift.

Knowledge of Your Culture's History

The more accurate your knowledge of your culture's history, the more aware you are of reality. If you rely instead on tradition, your perspective will be distorted. It can be a difficult trap to avoid because all cultures and many leaders like to put themselves at the center of the universe and then rewrite history to suit their purposes: "We dominate the industry. We control the infrastructure." This phenomenon is a form of ethnocentrism—evaluating others according to one's own values and traditions. It produces distorted histories of nations, leaders, and organizations. The danger in this is that if you are told something often enough, it begins to be real. Eventually, we come to believe our own stories.

After World War II, for example, many of America's business leaders deluded themselves into thinking they would face little competition from nations whose economies had been destroyed. After all, America had conquered all; it deserved to be "the greatest." Not enough thought was given to the likelihood that those war-torn economies would not only be rebuilt, but with modern structures. When Germany, Japan, Korea, Taiwan, France, Italy, and Britain did recover from their losses of manpower and industrial capacity, the picture changed dramatically. America was jolted out of a complacent slumber, during which many unwise organizational, labor, and management practices had taken root.

Managers should always be alert for signs that their companies are falling victim to corporate ethnocentrism. Make sure you know the history of your organization, including its workforce and its market. Then make yourself aware of how outsiders perceive the same set of facts.

Resilience

It may be an oversimplification to say that life requires an ability to bounce back, but it does, and it helps you keep your perspective. President Clinton, a master at this, likened himself to the Baby Huey inflatable doll: "It's big, it's ugly, but when you knock it down, it comes right back up." Resilience is our best response to the anger and rigidity that are generated in the stressful times of change.

Entrepreneurs and those with what I call "menagerie minds" create resilience by always being immersed in a variety of projects and interests. They never depend on only one way to energize themselves, solve a problem, or earn a living. They seem able, when confronted with barriers, to quickly redirect their neurons into a new path. In effect, they can rewire their own circuits because they have such a diverse tool kit.

Resilient managers and companies accept mistakes and learn from them. Sam Walton of Wal-Mart was known for his resilience. When he or someone else botched something, he was never angry or embarrassed. He would simply return the next day, ready with a new idea or a new way to solve the problem. Richard Branson of the Virgin Group is an entrepreneur who hates negativity, so each "down" in his career quickly produces an "up." Resilient people like him are open and unguarded; they know how to let go of a problem and cut their losses. Then they come back at it again from a new perspective. They enjoy the process as much as the goal.

Multiple Sources of Information

Perspective requires you to look for information in all the unfamiliar places. Don't just read your favorite publications. Read at least one newspaper beyond your hometown and one international publication. Scan for information where you drive, park, shop, or play. Riding the bus or train exposes you to different populations. Eat at new restaurants in different areas with someone other than your regular companions. Listen to a different radio station, attend ethnic festivals and other churches. Put yourself outside your ordinary range.

This may sound like more information overload, but being trapped in the same old ideas is what causes us to drone out. New ideas expand our perspective. After all, perspective is like your body or your mind: You must stretch it or lose it.

Attention to the Repressed

Peter Senge, describing his experience with Harvard professor Chris Argyris in an informal workshop, wrote in *The Fifth Discipline*: "Argyris asked each of us to recount a conflict with a client, colleague, or family member. We had to recall not only what was said, but what we were thinking and did *not* say."[4] How often do you hold back your knowledge of a product or management weakness, and from whom? This exercise gets at an important truth: that what we do not say can become a defensive routine that eventually governs our behavior and perceptions.

Begin noticing what you do not say or allow yourself to think about, what you avoid or do not let yourself do. Experiment with breaking through your instinctive or reflexive resistance. It's easy with new food or new art. It is much harder in business relationships. The new 180-degree, work-evaluation processes require you to ask others in your organization what they think about you.

High Tolerance for Chaos

The ability to cope with confusion or ambivalence is important to nurturing perspective. Be tolerant of the eccentric, the erratic, the inconsistent, and what seems to be the misfiring of your own synapses. The intuitive mistakes of the body or mind are often the opening of a window to a new idea.

Even a staid publication like *The Economist* tells us: "Economic growth stems from corporate turbulence, not stagnation." Kevin Kelly, executive editor of *Wired*, compares equilibrium or balance with death. Do not stay on a success plateau too long, unless you need a rest. Avoid too much satisfaction, keep enough stress in your system to hold you upright without losing control. Learn to live with chaos.

Chaos theorists try to explain the complex and unpredictable patterns that underlic irregular change: weather, the roll of dice, financial markets, the body's own rhythms.[5] Chaos is irregularity. But the chaos adherents peer into this irregularity and see a pattern to it, a new order of sorts. In their minds, chaos perception is a way to look at the broader nature of things to find connectors. It is an awareness of process. Chaos, creativity, vision, and strategy go hand in hand.

The Ability to Insulate Your Hot Buttons

Our personalities and organizations are bristling with hot buttons that cause minds to snap shut when people say or do certain things. Hot buttons are barriers to reality, usually rooted in defensiveness or beliefs from the past. Remember the first black/white movie kisses, the first female film director, the Japanese purchase of the Pebble Beach golf course, Yitzhak Rabin and Yasser Arafat shaking hands, the O. J. Simpson verdict? We reacted emotionally to these situations or images because they pushed our hot buttons.

It is hard not to react. The mind fixes deeply a belief that generates emotional intensity, and a hot button is created. It becomes easier to imagine going to the moon than having a gay president. That is why parents, priests, and coaches have such powerful impacts on our thought systems: They teach in emotional environments.

Hot buttons can be passed down through generations. They break up families and teams, isolate executives, hobble managers, and create corporate environments in which everyone lies to everyone else. How to combat them? Managers have to get past issues of control, accountability, and risk. Workers have to learn to handle change, new colleagues, new rules, and lost expectations. In our society and private lives we have to get past "It's always been like that" or "It's not fair to change the rules now" or "I deserve what I have."

Pay attention when you get a visceral hit—that is, when your stomach jumps—at work, reading the paper, at home, talking to someone, whenever. Catch it, write it down, check it out. What is it, where did it come from? Were you taught this, did you inherit it, does it still make sense, could you let it go? Is it important to hold on to it?

If you have trouble recognizing your hot buttons—your biases and fears, in other words—ask your colleagues, friends, and spouse for help. They will have no trouble listing them for you. You need to understand the shaping and response of your old mind to generate a new one.

The Ability to Empathize

Perspective is naturally limited by personal experiences. By that I mean that we tend to see the world of others through our own lenses and our own experiences. Few things that we witness seem to make much of an impression on us unless they somehow relate to what we care about. Witnessing a dramatic event or a crisis in someone else's life can momentarily shake us out of this narrowness. But for a lasting improvement, we need to sharpen our day-to-day ability to empathize with others. It is what gives rise to the "walk in another person's shoes" advice. The ability to empathize helps us understand differences between ourselves and our neighbors or coworkers.

Books and films try to convey the experience of being someone else. *Black Like Me,* written by John Howard Griffen, tried to give whites a sense of the African-American experience by chronicling the abuses suffered by a white man who chemically darkened his skin. Others have written about pretending to be an old woman or a homeless person. *The Doctor* was a film about the doctor as patient. *Switch* was a film about a man who becomes a woman; *Big* about a boy who becomes a man.

In some schools, teachers divide elementary students into two groups—the "brown eyes," which are privileged, and the "blue eyes," which are underprivileged—so that they may experience the emotions of discrimination. Medical students are put into hospital gowns and subjected to a battery of diagnostic tests so they will be more aware of how patients feel.

There is a deep need for these exercises in corporate human relations and customer service programs. In any organization, even a momentary experience in someone else's position will broaden the perspective of managers and employees alike. It may be the only way to understand basic human conflict. Without direct experience, anything you say about those who are significantly different from you is an illusion. You are just making it up.

Time to Visualize

Some people have the ability, in a dreamlike way, to create a mental picture of a new product or process. These visualizations are always fuzzy at first. Their creators know but they don't know. Visualization aids perspective and creativity because it allows the mind to synthesize. But it requires that you give yourself time to wander mentally. Let your mind float and then hold on to the images and ideas that appear, trying at the same time to sharpen your vision of what will emerge at the end of the process.

The first employees of Microsoft imagined a computer at the desk of every student and an art museum in every home computer. They are now selling educational software, and they have bought the video rights to many art collections.

Techies use the term *vaporware* to describe the products of visualization. Vaporware is generated when an idea just pops out of your head or mouth, a spontaneous revelation. One of my favorite vaporware creations is "airwrite"—a large screen that I imagine as a stand-up computer for writers. Airwrite works like an old-fashioned felt storyboard. The writer stands there and edits or moves words with his or her hands. New words are added by voice recognition. This is whole-body, hands-on editing. You can dance and write, no more tight-body repetitive-motion injuries. Imagine aerobic writing, the sensuality of embracing the words, touching the images they form.

Visualization helps me get past work problems. When I'm stuck, I get up and go out to my garden. As I walk around, I begin to mentally rearrange the landscape. After a while, I usually get an image of what I want, but my hands at first don't quite know how to do it. I move a few rocks or plants and wait for my mind to make the right connections. When I return to my work inside, I have usually solved the work problem and begun to solve the garden problem.

When you're stuck, get out of your office, home, or wherever you are. You can do it through your mind by taking a nap, reading something, or watching a movie, but it helps to move your body as well. Sterile offices without windows shut down the imagination. You can improve your perspective by just standing up.

Perspective is often the first casualty in periods of rapid change. Tugged in opposite directions by a familiar present and an uncertain future, we can lose our balance and our ability to keep things in perspective. But it doesn't have to be that way. We can learn to recognize the many factors that may be distorting our perceptions. We can sharpen our perspective skills. In short, we can keep our eyes and minds open to the forces of change as they will affect our businesses and our lives.

Recognizing the Future

"As willing as he was to do impromptu magic with their questions, he did not seem interested in devoting his own research to any problem that might pay off. He thought about turbulence in liquids and gases. He thought about time—did it glide smoothly forward—or hop discretely like a sequence of cosmic motion-picture frames? He thought about the eye's ability to see consistent colors and forms in a universe that physicists knew to be a shifting quantum kaleidoscope. He thought about clouds, watching them from airplane windows (until his flight privileges were suspended on grounds of overuse) or from hiking trails above the laboratory."

—JAMES GLEICK DESCRIBING MITCHELL FEIGENBAUM,
THE DISCOVERER OF UNIVERSAL THEORY,
IN *CHAOS: THE MAKING OF A NEW SCIENCE*

P ATTERNS ARE MENTAL MAPS that can lead us to visionary ideas. Geniuses like Feigenbaum, using their knowledge of natural law and their intuition, actually create new patterns. Most of us are not in the genius category, but we can at least train ourselves like good detectives to notice when patterns are changing—in our lives, in our work, and in the world markets.

There are patterns beneath our current confusion. The trick is to develop an eye for bits of information or clues that, when assembled, present us with a new and visible pattern or trend. I use *pattern* and *trend* interchangeably. Both trends and patterns are simply sequences of events, ideas, or forms of behavior that have economic, social, or political significance. Every manager needs to be aware of patterns if he or she is to track changes in products and markets. This means developing the analytical and intuitive skills necessary to recognize a new pattern and determine whether it is a harbinger of genuine change. Some new patterns are just brief fads, but others are long-term trends worth millions. The successful manager needs to be able to tell the difference. The payoff is the ability to anticipate change, not just follow it.

That is what the Japanese did so well in the 1980s. They did not create; they recognized the appearance of a pattern in the development of products such as quartz watches, active matrix flat screens, and memory chips. Their understanding of that pattern and its implications soon enabled them to dominate particular markets, often by buying patents and research expertise elsewhere. You don't have to be an inventor to be successful, but you do have to notice the inventions of others.

Patterns always seem logical in hindsight. The problem is detecting them—and understanding their importance—while they are still taking shape. Think how difficult it is to fully appreciate what might result from a new invention. The steam engine, for example, was invented to pump water out of mines. Inventor Marconi thought radio would be useful only in ship-to-shore situations, where stringing a wire or cable was impossible. Early commentators saw the main use of broadcast radio as limited to Sunday sermons because that was the only time they could think of when one person addressed a large audience.

Picking up the right trends may be as important for a manager as producing quality products or excelling in customer service. You know the stories. Bell Labs did not see the application of its invention of the laser to the telephone business. American electronics companies missed the fax revolution; they did not marry telephones to printers until Japan had taken over the market. IBM decided in 1949 not to bother with personal computers because it believed that world demand could be satisfied with ten to fifteen mainframe machines.

Timing is everything when it comes to trends. Companies that move too soon (Sony's Beta-format videotapes, People's Express Airline) miss the wave that others (Neopath, the creator of automated Pap tests, Southwest Airlines) time perfectly. Companies that enter the market too late (Logan Drive, Coffee People) don't catch much of a wave because the competition (The Gap, Starbucks) got there first. Timing is harder than trying to judge whether the wave is going to be too small to bother with (eight-tracks, mechanical bulls, cigars). You have to be in position before the wave breaks.

Think about today's familiar consumer trends: soft drinks, sports shoes, fast food, frozen entrées, and warehouse shopping. The best way to capitalize now on one of these mature trends is to create a successful variation (Ben & Jerry's Ice Cream, New York Seltzer, Snapple) or to steal someone's customers with a cheaper or better product. Today's declining trends are equally familiar: chemical lawn care, department stores, tobacco, fur. If you are working in an area you even suspect is a declining trend, get out.

Were you able to spot these growing trends: healthcare products, continuing education, gardening, home delivery, catalog shopping, fish farms, home health care, maintenance services, and security or alarm systems and related products? Some new trends to watch are spiritual products and services, communal living, electronic banking, pay-per-view home entertainment, crafts, environmentally sensitive products, plastic surgery, cancer treatment centers, solar energy, voice-activation technology, and child care.

You should be aware of how any new trend will affect your business or organization. You should also be able to spot new channels of distribution and marketing and their effects: interactive telemarketing, multimedia event spin-offs (products as entertainment), fewer face-to-face transactions, more warehouses, more catalogs, more expert sources for new products (*PC* magazine, *Photography* magazine). How will you buy a car in the year 2000? You will use your computer to access all models, consumer ratings, and prices. A dealer will then bring your top three choices to your house for a test drive, and you'll never set foot in a showroom.

DRIVING FORCES

Four basic trends are driving the development of almost all new products today: increasing complexity and customization, miniaturization, multitasking, and our growing interest in the adaptability of mind and body. How to create goods and services that respond to the "techie" trends as well as to the quest for "holistic" living is a complicated challenge for any company.

The increasing complexity of all of our technologies and tastes is obvious. Even so, there is a new intimacy between supplier and consumer that may become the norm. Marriott keeps a record of what newspaper or kind of fruit its frequent guests want in their rooms. Customization will be reflected not just in new products and services designed with individual customers in mind, but in the creation of new organizational structures to make or supply them (British business guru Charles Handy suggests a clover leaf to replace the pyramid, MIT management professor Peter Senge suggests an orchestra or chorus).

Miniaturization will influence everything. Its most dramatic impact thus far is in electronics and communications technology. A strand of glass (fiber optics) thinner than a human hair can transmit a full-length motion picture in a fraction of a second. A single silicon chip can hold 50 million transistors or a billion bits of information, allowing entire data systems to fit within a space that is one inch square.

Computers that are pocket size or fit on the wrist come with tiny windowlike screens that display the equivalent of what is seen on full twelve-inch screens. The information appears to be floating in space. Reflection Technology markets these miniature computers under the name Private Eye. Casio markets a television in a beer can, the Can-Tele, with a one-inch screen.

Nanotechnology—miniaturization to microscopic size, one billionth of a meter—is next. *Nano* is from the Greek word for "dwarf." One day we will be able to manipulate individual atoms. Science writer James Gleick speculates that we may send "nanobots" through the bloodstream to clean out cholesterol deposits or battle viruses. In his book, *The Future*, Ronald Rotstein describes scientists at Bell Laboratories working with a .005-inch-diameter turbine engine that is the size of a decimal point. "You have to be careful when handling these things," one scientist told him. "I've accidentally inhaled a few right into my lungs."[1]

Multitasking, the ability to do many things at once, is already a way of life. Long ago, for example, the farmer's combine replaced a team of horses and men. Now our machines do increasing numbers of things. The telephone has metamorphosed into automatic dialer, recorder, desktop speaker, message taker, fax, copier, and bank. Microsoft's Windows 95 software fills a computer screen with icons that signal it is ready to perform nearly every task required to run a life or a business.

Our growing interest in mind and body maintenance and adaptation has obvious implications for food products. The old question about food was "Will I get enough to eat?" Remember the clean-plate club and other food tortures at the dinner table? Now the question for Americans is "Is this the right thing to eat?" Red meat might eventually become a condiment, a garnish, served in small portions or reserved for special occasions. Other reversals are already in sight.

The carbos are winning; vegetables and legumes are not far behind. Tacos have surpassed pizza. The nineties may be the broccoli decade. The nutrition requirements for a longer, more sedentary life are known and will eventually become the norm. If you want to live to be one hundred, you have to eat lower on the food chain. When we're stressed, of course, the old habits sometimes return. Nutritionist Ahmed Kissebah called it the "civilization syndrome." A piece of meat after a hard day was the reward of a hunter, and we still feed, sometimes, like tired hunters.

Big-game hunting used to be a way of survival; a successful hunt was a time for celebration. Now the taking of a whale is greeted with grief. Deer hunters are confronted by their children holding up Bambi signs. Their spouses don't want to eat venison or wear trapped fur. Veal is taboo because the calf did not have a full life before being turned into cutlets. A minimal meat diet is gaining in appeal as we increasingly support nonviolence toward any living animal. Turtle-free shrimp and free-range-chicken breasts are mind-boggling concepts. As we become more mechanized, we feel more intensely protective of nature.

Changes like these do not happen all at once; our unconscious impulses are too strong for that. We will long prefer the sensual pleasures of food rich in fat and sugar, regardless of what we learn about nutrition. We will long fear things that were dangerous in a wild environment (snakes, spiders, darkness) more than those that are far more dangerous in our urban environment (machines, cars, guns). As life grows more complex, we will long for what we imagine was simple.

PREDICTING CHANGE

We can dig deeper into the ways to understand patterns and predict change. Here are six processes through which patterns evolve. I call them *extension, elaboration, recycling, pattern reversals, strange attractions,* and *chaos.* Understanding these processes can provide the "aha" of hindsight in advance.

Extension

When you observe a known condition, phenomenon, or practice and imagine how it might continue to develop or expand—and with what implications—that is the process of extension. It is probably the easiest way to predict patterns and trends. For example, if one type of business stays open twenty-four hours a day, why not others?

Another example of extension would be to follow up on the baby-boom bulge. What do the boomers need now? They need skin care, plastic surgery, vitamins, health care, drugs, exercise, retirement plans, and funerals. They want to read books such as *Embracing the Light* and *How We Die.* But don't stop with the boomers. Think how our life spans in general are increasing. Healthier habits and biomedical breakthroughs have already extended average life expectancy from forty-seven in 1900 to eighty in 1996. What if we add another thirty years in the decades ahead? An aging population will value time, comfort, health, and recreation. What impact will an aging population have on your business or livelihood?

Every change in transportation, from horse-drawn carts to automobiles and airplanes, has affected the way our society is organized. Residence, work, and production patterns have shifted with each of these advances. What's next? And how will it affect social patterns? The Moller 400 is a levitation vehicle invented by Paul Moller. It seats four, takes off vertically, can do 400 miles an hour, hovers low, lands softly, and parks in your garage. The world's fastest train, Transrapid, glides between Berlin and Hamburg at 280 miles per hour using magnetic levitation.

Try the extension process with energy sources. Push beyond traditional sources of power, beyond even nuclear, to hydrogen-based energy. Imagine the effect on your business or your life if all the countries of the world with access to water could vaporize it into fuel for homes, businesses, and transportation. Or for a more familiar example, flash back to the impact of the electric light. It ended the regime of night and day, of indoors and outdoors.

At first, few people were conscious of the important pattern that was taking shape. I still remember when all stores closed at 6:00 P.M. and all television programs stopped at 11:00 P.M. with a fluttering flag and the national anthem. Now, at least in the cities, we can do virtually everything twenty-four hours a day, 365 days a year. This time-and-light revolution, augmented now by electronic technology, is still gathering momentum.

The personal computer industry, only two decades old, is a lesson in how rapidly and unexpectedly the shape of a pattern can extend—especially where technology is involved. At the outset, the industry imagined everyone with a computer. But the first software was too difficult and too filled with bugs for the anxious user. Making matters worse, almost nobody foresaw how swiftly computer technology would advance, rendering many of the early expensive machines obsolete in a relatively short time. The real market for personal computers in the 1980s turned out to be in the business world, where both motivation and training were available and the benefits far outweighed the hassles. Later, of course, the pattern changed again, and computers did explode into the home market.

When we become comfortable with a pattern, we often make the mistake of assuming that it will remain static. So we fail to look at its potential for extension. Businesses do this all the time. Telephone companies did not imagine that the science that enabled them to transmit electronic pulses through lines would evolve to the point where no lines would be necessary, but Craig McCaw, founder of McCaw Cellular, did. AT&T knew the possibilities of cellular telephones from experiments being conducted in its labs. But it ignored, for too long, how neatly these devices might fit into an already recognized pattern: our increasing mobility. Similarly, communications executives were unprepared for the extraordinary rise in overseas telephone traffic, although a pattern of increased business activity between the United States and foreign companies was evident. Telephone companies also overlooked the danger that cable TV operators would elbow their way into providing communication services. When someone else is hanging wires on your poles, it has to be competition. So many businesses—and even nations—continue to believe that they control a vital infrastructure or resource when they don't. Reality sinks in at about the time that change virtually runs them over.

Extension can help us project where technology is going. Look at what might happen when the concept of communicating with a machine is extended beyond voice mail. At home or work, computerized systems will respond to your verbal demand for help or pick up and delivery. Your car will tell you when it needs service: "Burton, I'm feeling some tension in my U-joint." Computers married to television sets will generate animated characters or icons in the corner of your screen to remind you when the shows you like are coming on. They will even call your attention to a related program that might appeal to you and give you summaries or reruns of programs you missed. Want to create your own program lineup? They will do that for you, too.

Meanwhile, in the deep of the night, machines will load and wash your dishes, fold your laundry, vacuum, dust, cook your food, and water the houseplants. (We already have telephones with temperature and humidity sensors that call you if the house gets hot, cold, or wet.) The next morning, autopiloted transportation will let you sleep on the way to work. Eventually, these voice-activated agents—the HAL of *2001*, with charm—will function like stockbrokers, post offices, travel agents, ticket offices, librarians, or accountants.

Extension can work for people who do something now that they want to do better. Micro Dexterity Systems provides an example: a modification of the surgeon's hand. The creator, Dr. Steve Charles, an eye specialist, envisions a mechanical arm, fused with the surgeon's, that would take the wobble out of the scalpel. A logical extension for almost everything is how to make it faster, smarter, cleaner, safer.

Extension is also a way to take note of other life-forms and speculate about how we might adapt some of their most important skills or attributes. If owls can see at night, couldn't man find a way to do that, too? Plant seeds taught us about aerodynamics and Velcro. Mosquitoes taught us about drawing blood. Birds in flight suggested the design of hang gliders.

One of the most intense areas of extension stems from our desire to expand our senses. We've done it with vision (telescopes, microscopes, X-rays, contact lenses, radial keratotomies, lasers), hearing (hearing aids, implants, ultrasound, sonar devices, stethoscopes, synthesizers), smell (scented products, scratch-and-sniff, pheromones, aromatherapy), taste (proliferation of food products, artificial flavors and sweeteners), and touch (robotics, sensors, virtual reality, electronic massage). What's the next step?

THE NET

Look at communications—in particular, the Internet—to see the most important example today of a pattern that is being extended. The familiar communications links—letters, books, newspapers, magazines, films, and television—always told a few stories to many people. On the Internet, for the first time in history, many people tell many stories to many other people. Twenty million people worldwide are on "the net," creating on-line interest groups, friendships, and even romances. Ham radio operators went to great expense and spent long hours to reach around the world. The net lets you do it at your computer in seconds.

When a friend of mine was diagnosed with pancreatic cancer, he located "Oncolink" through the "mosaic" information system and found a support group for his type of cancer and a review of the latest treatment. The next day he was in touch via electronic mail with a surgeon involved in an experimental cryosurgery project, his case files were faxed, and he was on a plane. Within forty-eight hours of diagnosis, he was being prepped for surgery. The cancer turned out to be too widespread to control, and he was sent home. Now he logs into an around-the-clock pancreatic cancer support group and gets comfort from friends or help with nausea in the middle of the night from an herbalist in Taiwan he has never met. This is not an impersonal world. It is global intimacy.

The net has already become an infrastructure for synthesizing, storing, and distributing information. On the net, you will be able to learn more about a new drug your doctor prescribed or find out what government records have to say about you. Computer bulletin boards with recommendations from fellow users will help you evaluate the reputation of professionals or craftsmen when you need their services. This informal exchange, a lot like the neighborhood bulletin boards of the past, will be far more powerful than celebrities hawking goods on QVC. Some scientists are already abandoning their professional journals to discuss research findings with colleagues on the Internet—in effect, instant, cutting-edge, worldwide seminars.

Computers and their networks are connecting more and more brains and sending faster and faster pulses between them. Advertisers, according to *The Wall Street Journal*, have already identified this market as the "techno-savvies." Here is a sampling of some of the extensions that lie ahead. Will you or your company be able to take advantage of them?

Computer home shopping—Ordering from a catalog via computer with automatic cost comparisons, similar to what you see on per-unit pricing labels on supermarket shelves. You type in the message "I need yellow sheets." The computer tells you the closest stores that have them and compares quality, price, availability, shipping time, and even the *Consumer Reports* "best buy" evaluation. UPS delivers the sheets in the morning.

Voice Mail Plus—A combination of answering machine and voice mail. Listen:

> *Ringgggg.*
> VMP: Sasha's line.
> Pete: Hi, is there a message for Pete from Sasha?
> VMP: Sasha said that if you called that, yes, she would love to see you. Please bring the book she lent you last week. Choose your time between six and eight P.M. and the place you prefer to meet. See you then. To change your mind, press seven. To listen to Sasha's thought for the day, press eight.

Health Guard Plus—Your entire health history is coded on a card and updated automatically each time you change a prescription, have an accident, get an illness, or have a checkup. In an emergency, the card—interacting with diagnostic equipment—will recommend treatment.

Smart Guns—Sandia National Laboratories is exploring guns that are intelligent enough to fire only if activated by the authorized user. The technology includes magnetic rings on the grip, fingerprint, palm print, and voice-activated sensors.

EXTENSION OF ALMOST EVERYTHING

Traditional companies have a hard time with obvious extensions—for example, the expansion of a customer base—when they violate previously agreed-upon limits. Kraft General Foods pulled its commercials from the episode of *Roseanne* in which she received a surprise lesbian kiss from Mariel Hemingway. American Express bought the time and created a new commercial to advertise its Cheques for Two—with names clearly indicating that the traveler's checks had been purchased by same-sex couples. Kraft had also pulled its commercials from programs dealing with masturbation and racism. Whom does that leave to buy their products?

It is hard to know where to draw the line in new markets. (Subaru of America, the Travelers Bank, and Visa U.S.A. are teaming up with tennis star Martina Navratilova.) Changing awareness of sexual choices is a long-term pattern that will continue to prod our ambivalence. We're talking techno-sex—another example of the extension of communication patterns. We've had telephone sex for decades. Now it's possible to sign onto a computer bulletin board late on a Saturday night, contact a "date," and get to know each other.

Electronic communication is expanding in countless directions. Nobody knows the limits. There are already battles over ethics, censorship, and freedom of speech. Cyberpunks, like all punks, are pushing the limits, high on electronic vibrations. It's the cyberspace equivalent of the Wild West. On the frontier, "boys" are brawling, taking potshots at each other on Main Street. But communities sooner or later create rules and norms to civilize and expand the use of any new technology.

Elaboration

Elaboration is the process of modifying, further developing, or perfecting an existing product or service. Elaboration is the best way to capitalize on an already established pattern or trend. The Japanese have done it better than anyone else with automobiles and home electronics. The Sony Walkman kept defeating its clones because Sony stayed one jump ahead. Each new version was smaller, lighter, used less energy, was more reliable, had a more comfortable headset, and cost less.

Engineered food is an elaboration of a common pattern: improving the size, quality, growing time, and nutritional content of plants and animals. When we were kids, we used to play at inventing foods, like corn crossed with carrots so you could eat the cob, or Brussels sprouts with a Tootsie Pop center to make them more appetizing. Now adults do it, but on a grander scale, through the science of genetic engineering. Beta III is a supercarrot with twice the vitamin A of a regular carrot. On the farm, genetically identical calves are bred for a particular trait that adds value to the animal. Fish are farmed with an interesting twist: The reproductive process is altered with a hormone to produce mainly females. They grow faster, fight less, and taste better, according to the experts. Oysters are being sterilized so they will direct all their energies into growth. Eventually captive birds and bees may no longer "do it." We humans, of course, have also been elaborating on our own reproduction technologies, including insemination for single women, in vitro fertilization, embryo implants, and gender selection. This manipulation of reproduction will have long-term implications for our mating and sex patterns.

Other patterns that lend themselves to elaboration are the basics of competition and marketing. For example, two kids have side-by-side lemonade stands. Cassandra offers a bigger glass for the same price. Ryan adds more ice. Cassandra offers a colored straw and a slice of fruit. Ryan adds a coupon system that enables the customer to get one lemonade free. Cassandra introduces discounts for friends and family. At that point, their parents call it quits and drag them into the house. The mid-nineties explosion of espresso carts is a sequel to the lemonade stands of a slower time.

Disney built vacation resorts around entertainment and product sales. Now shopping malls are adding entertainment to their merchandising mix. Advertising is a complex elaboration of what was once a simple message painted on a store front or barn. Now people wear ads, sit on ads, or view ads on billboards that move, smoke, or steam. Cereal boxes talk in point-of-purchase displays, which are among the fastest growing advertising venues.

Elaboration can also mean broadening the focus of a product or service, or expanding its range. Look at all the forms of a generic item such as oatmeal: from the ordinary stuff to instant to individual servings to flavored varieties to microwavable. But let's not stop there. If we keep elaborating, we might devise even more customized formulas, like those currently available in dog food. How about oatmeal for students or athletes or tired adults or pregnant women or the constipated or the overweight—each individually formulated and discretely labeled?

Supermarket shelves cannot accommodate all the marketable product variations. But we played out the elaboration process and came up with computerized warehouses that could do the job. Imagine shoppers without carts, holding keypads or scanners as they stroll through real or video aisles. At the checkout counter, their goods will already be bagged and waiting.

My array of oatmeal seems absurd until you remember that the marketing specialists at PRIZM (Potential Rating Index by ZIP Market), once content with nine categories of American consumers in 1980, now list sixty-two. The newest PRIZM groups include "Kids and Cul-de-sacs" (new immigrants), "Cashmere and Country Clubs" (aging, wealthy, suburban baby-boomers), and "New Ecotopia" (aging hippies). PRIZM was founded on the theory that birds of a feather flock together, but the flocks are getting more numerous as our interests diversify. The demand for variety, the multiplication of niches, and the endless possibilities for new versions of a product will not slow down or simplify. The best way to cope may be to try to imagine the next niche consumer group for your product or service. I already have my favorites: "Burned-out Liberal Downsizers" shop at Costco. "Tight-time Upscale Frantics" prefer catalogs. "Money and Brains Hackers" read *Byte* or *Wired*, not *Esquire*.

Air travel is a service that will continue to elaborate. It must find ways to lure the business traveler, who can now stay at home if he or she has a "technological cottage." Thus the installation of telephones; screens with news, sports, and movies; and vibrating massagers at every first- and business-class seat. Aircraft compartments that can reconfigure quickly—with movable seats—are increasingly important. Techies will carry computers that chart flights and gates and map out strategy for switching reservations, making connections, and securing the best seats. They will operate like a Gameboy to see if the traveler, the airline, or the weather wins.

Look around you. What part of your business or service can be elaborated? At what point is an elaborated version positive and when does it tip to the negative? If your market is static or shrinking, is there some elaboration that would enlarge it?

Recycling

Recycling is the familiar process whereby an old pattern or trend makes a comeback, either because we are nostalgic for it or because there is a new generation to intrigue with old successes. Popcorn has made a big comeback, as have fountain pens, vests, and heavy boots. You can generate many "new" products and services just by knowing about the old ones. We regularly revive hits such as the Slinky and squirt guns. You can even bring back a flop, if the time is right. All the forms of "goo" come back. Bears, trolls, and gargoyles are always being recycled. Tiddlywinks or mumbletypegs came back as Pog, a game using disks of various designs. Is there some aspect of your business that could be revived to take advantage of recycling patterns or trends?

Pattern Reversals

Reversals in patterns or trends are the normal playing out of the tension between opposites. When we push too far in one direction, there is a tendency for whatever we are pushing to snap back. Veggie burgers somehow create a demand for steak houses. Women's business suits are worn over underwear from the Victoria's Secret catalog.

It is very difficult for even a powerful trend to develop without interruption or momentary reactions in the other direction. Because our minds prefer order, we like to pretend that the direction is always forward, despite evidence to the contrary. In truth, there are usually many hesitations along the way. I call it the "dance of life," two steps forward and one step back. The step back provides a breathing spell, a chance to stabilize, and at first may seem like a total reversal, but it is not. It is only hesitation, and the actual trend over a longer period of time will be forward, despite the hesitations.

When the trends are especially complex, we often

react by trying to simplify. The more capable doctors and hospitals become at prolonging life, the more people want to take back control and die in their own way at home. High-tech hospital delivery rooms with complex monitoring equipment have given rise to birthing rooms with soft lights, music, and rocking chairs. People flee the cities to live in log cabins (albeit with indoor plumbing). If a trend is particularly strong, there will be in all probability a reaction to it, which may provide an opportunity or niche market for your company.

Strange Attractions

Strange attractions are odd combinations of patterns or trends that seem unpredictable. They have a self-organizing order that we cannot easily discover, like clouds, swirling liquids, or cracks in glass, yet often make sense in retrospect. The Teenage Mutant Ninja Turtles were a bizarre combination of heroic turtles, the martial arts, and Zen values that, upon reflection, was understandable as an amalgamation of other trends.

The "grunge" fashion wave, plaid shirts and baggy pants on middle-class kids in the 1990s, does not seem as strange when we remember the hippie styles of the 1960s; both were reactions to the uptight expectations of the preceding decades. Unusual combinations are another form of strange attractions. At the Nature Company, techies buy geodes and crystals to put on top of their computers—a way to make their electronic surroundings earthy. L. L. Bean outerwear shares closet space with tailored three-piece business suits and pastel Hush Puppies.

Chaos

The biggest mistake we can make in trying to predict patterns and trends is to have too narrow a focus. Chaos, or order without surface predictability, cautions us against that. Scientists are warning that the closer we get to thinking we understand and can control a pattern, the more likely we are to be surprised when it turns out to be quite different from what we imagined.

Chaos explains the unpredictability of complex forms. It is the pattern that most resembles human adaptation. Think how we can spontaneously generate, like a kaleidoscope, eternally creative arrangements. Artificial intelligence relies on an understanding of the order of chaos.

Much of the computer software market is now in chaos because there are so few fixed parameters. In 1995 IBM paid $3.5 billion for Lotus Development Corporation because it believed it would then dominate the software market for internal or local business connections that Lotus "Notes" had established. But software development for organizing the "Intranet" (information exchanges between computers in the same net) is too wide-open for such a big investment. Netscape already has competing connecting software, and Microsoft just released its new product, Exchange.

Chaos theory is the science of process, the knowledge of what is becoming, not what is or will remain. Our minds and our businesses are not always systems in balance; they are always in process. Just try to trace a thought or a conversation back to its genesis. Do the same with your business product or service. What was it, what is it now, what is it likely to become? If you allow your mind to play with even unlikely possibilities in relation to some current pattern or trend, the future will not come as a surprise.

THE CHARACTERISTICS OF ENTREPRENEURIAL MINDS

We live in the age of the entrepreneur, those innovative men and women who can spot patterns and trends, and seize opportunities that others miss. Here are some of the characteristics that entrepreneurial minds have applied in business and the products or services that were the result.

Serendipity—An aptitude for making use of accidental discoveries (*Teflon*).

Flexibility—The ability to change your business to accommodate new customers (*golf carts in airports*).

Ingenuity—The ability to think freely and openly, clever and original thought; a characteristic also known as "coincidental adaptation" (*Netscape*).

Niche picking—The ability to spot what customers want that you can do faster, cheaper, and better (*Hooked on Phonics*).

Fast footwork and multiple agendas—The ability to follow the "corridor principle"—once you are in an established business, you see the next door and move through it faster than the competition (*First Direct electronic bank*).

New channels—The ability to notice and exploit expanded or new distribution channels (airline catalogs, ATMs in gas stations, Southwestern Bell stores in supermarkets).

Hypothetical thought—The ability to reevaluate an existing product and ask these questions: Should the size, color, shape, or material be changed? Can it be made to last longer or should it be thrown away sooner? (*Tetra pack square juice box*).

Comparative thinking or application—The ability to see what other companies are already doing successfully, something that your product or service could benefit from (*Costco, Office Depot, Pet Mart*).

Radical thinking—The ability to make a complete departure from existing approaches or take a 180-degree turn to see if flipping the problem will solve it (*Gateway Computer*).

PATTERN SKILLS

Developing the ability to recognize patterns and trends will do more than enable you to catch the next product line or beat out the competition. As our lives become more complex, that ability will enable you to anticipate or imagine the future. Here are some ideas that will start you on the way to tapping into that power.

Tracing—Take the most recent successful product or social movement you know about and backtrack through the processes that created it. Find out what went on in the originator's mind and follow the mental map.

The compact disk is an example. CDs were slow to arrive because everyone's model was the big LP. Initially, there was reluctance to go to a product that was smaller and denser, even though miniaturization was a major trend. A Norwegian created the CD, but the Japanese, familiar with miniaturization, saw the pattern and produced it.

MADD (Mothers Against Drunk Driving) has had an unusually rapid and far-reaching impact on American behavior and business. The grief that Candy Lightner felt when her daughter was killed cracked the old model of toleration for drinking and driving. The combination of an accumulation of pressure (drunk driving statistics) and a personal crusade made the difference.

Language—Language can be a signal that a pattern is developing. Notice words you use that are not in your computer spellcheck. Notice when new words pile up around a single product or topic area. Once a thing is named, it is far along in the development process. The more terms for something, the stronger its hold. The quick and rich taxonomy that developed around Internet culture (*cyberspace, wired, hyperlink, home page*) was a surefire indicator of its long-term value. The same kind of new language developed among the first computer buffs. The new language of teenagers has always been an indicator of their interests.

New mixes—Who lives in this country now and what are their beliefs and lifestyles? The United States Department of Commerce reports that we have doubled our monthly bill for communications links, prefer voice mail (58 percent) to dealing with a person (42 percent), work at home in significant numbers (43 percent), use our brains not our brawn (70 percent), and increasingly own personal computers (28 percent). Research on the behavior patterns of those who used to be called "nerds" holds some especially fascinating implications for American businesses. We have come full circle, and nerds are now "cool." They eat less meat, drink less milk or beer, prefer soft drinks and bottled water, have less interest than their fathers in contact sports, golf less, bowl more, don't gamble, and seldom hang out in bars. They don't dry-clean their clothes because they are more casual. They don't buy suits or dress shoes, and nerds of both sexes buy fewer clothes and spend less time shopping. They don't smoke, hunt, or eat much candy, but they do garden, raise exotic fish, and bird-watch.[2]

Obsolescence—Look around your storage areas. What have you stopped using? Look around the supermarket. What have you stopped buying? Do the same at the malls. What stores do you no longer enter and why? Read old newspapers and take note of industries, products, or companies that no longer exist. Think about the stores you grew up with. What happened? What changed?

I was in the San Francisco airport when I noticed a

small glassed-in room across from my gate. It looked like a holding cell. I walked over to take a look and realized it was the concourse smoking room. There was one lone man pacing in it. Poll takers report that Americans think smokers have lower IQs than nonsmokers. What is leaving the scene is as important as what is arriving.

Keep a journal—Most of us like to have data to back up our intuitive sense of a pattern. It gives us confidence in our judgment. Take any subject—a product, a service, or a personal interest—and record the number of times it is mentioned in the media. If there is other evidence of its existence or occurrence, note that, too. What are people talking about? What do they say they want or need? After a time, your journal will reveal a trend or pattern. This is what John Naisbitt did, over a period of years, to create his book *Megatrends*.

Ask basic questions. What is still a problem? Is there a solution?—Blood shortages (artificial blood, bloodless laser surgery), crime (microchip monitoring), weight issues (plastic food), transportation gridlock (navigation software), garbage (biodegradables), moods/mental health (psychoactive drugs), aging (spare parts and control of free radicals), information overload (computer "elves"), death (cryogenics, sperm, egg, and DNA banks), fertility (in vitro fertilization and embryo implants), lost children (locator chips), intelligence (smart drugs).

Maintain a menagerie mind—Let your mind loose so you can envision the not-so-obvious implications of a trend. Imagine combining products that would seem unlikely candidates for marriage. The menagerie mind is comfortable with incongruity, and that is what creates breakthroughs. The jumble of impulses that is our brain may just flash on a great idea one day. During my lectures, I sometimes find myself talking about a product or service as if it exists until people ask me where they can lay their hands on it. I, of course, have to confess that my own menagerie mind was synthesizing a lot of strands into whole cloth.

The mind is like a popcorn popper. You have to turn up the heat before something begins to happen. Imagination is what heats up the brain. Once you are open to imagining something, you can begin the process of creating it. Put words to concepts and the reality is only a moment away. One way you can test it is to ask if it conforms to current trends. The strength and longevity of your product or service will depend upon its depth and its connections to long-term cultural, social, and economic patterns. Pattern awareness will help you intuit the rhythms of growth and the direction of change. It is your crystal ball to see into the future.

Harnessing the Power of Myths and Symbols

"The meaning of a message is the change which it produces in the image."

—MARSHALL MCLUHAN

MYTHS ARE THE THREADS that link us to our past and shape our perception of the present. When we ask why our culture is the way it is and why we see things the way we do, the answer is usually found in these many-layered stories that we all unconsciously share. Although idealized and exaggerated, they represent our culture's deepest beliefs and perceptions.

While myths reinforce the bond between individuals in a group, they can also serve to separate one group from another. The Cold War, for example, was largely built on myths about the Communist bloc (it wasn't a bloc) and threat (it wasn't a genuine threat). Myths are so powerful that people live by them (religion), deny reality to believe in them (creationism versus evolution), and use them to justify discrimination (the belief that men are stronger than women). Governments and businesses base many of their decisions on myths, and so do we. Social scientists believe that everything we do bears the mark of the mythology of our culture, from what we eat and wear to whether our thinking is oriented toward the present or the future.

Myths set our schedules (Christians still rest on the

seventh day, others on the sixth). Myths provide models for productivity (Paul Bunyan and "The Little Engine That Could") and for ideals (Cinderella and Johnny Appleseed). Myths explain the events of our world. All societies have similar origin myths and many feature virgin birth.

The legends or stories that constitute myths can be clues to the way a culture views reality—or to the way it adapts its beliefs to *fit* reality. God became a father in the clouds with a beard because the image of the strong father seemed the most appropriate that real life had to offer at the dawn of Christianity.

Myths are at their most powerful when we are anxious. They attach themselves to all of life's crises, from birth (pain as a good thing) to marriage (the ideal of virginity) to death (heaven and Saint Peter). Myths even explain sudden good fortune (it was just our lucky day) and tragedy (it was God's or Allah's will). All advertising, of course, is largely myth. Cigarettes do not transport you to nature, beer does not produce beautiful women or good buddies, and cosmetics cannot guarantee beauty, youth, or a date. Even so, advertising's illusions mutate to become beliefs about sex and cigarettes, virility and beer, or hair color and social success.

Myths are survival tales, stories of heroes, of violence, of respect and honor. The rise of agriculture and then urban manufacturing meant that fewer men were required to herd or hunt, but the myths remain in games and rituals. The past echoes in lodges where men call themselves Knights, Eagles, Elk, and Moose; women are Moosettes and their children Moose Yearlings.

The power of the myth is such that most people are unable to separate what they believe into "this is myth" and "this is real." Myths get in the way of understanding what is happening around us. When we try to process new information about our lives or our work, we naturally filter it through our existing beliefs—including our full collection of myths. They cloud our perceptions, tap our emotions, and make it difficult to see reality.

Leaders who cannot separate old myth from new realities will join exclusive clubs, withdraw from their communities and employees, easily justify wage disparities, and remain unaware of the impact on production, perception, and worker morale. Managers will fail to hire women and minorities because they cannot see their qualifications. Young men unable to find jobs as timberworkers will become despondent because other ways of earning a living seem unmanly by comparison.

Political battles over timber, water, and air pit economic myths against environmental myths, and each side buys its own scientific expert. Mythical thinking doesn't just lead you to sell all your possessions and wait for the end of the world (if your guru has declared it is coming). It also affects your ability to run a business and maintain relationships. You assume others think like you when, in fact, they may have a different set of beliefs. Business myths are couched in sports metaphors to denote competitive spirit, just as athletic teams still call themselves Braves and Indians to denote their ferocity. Shootouts that gang members equate with masculinity and in-your-face politics as a leadership style are remnants of classic myths (gunfights and jousting).

Our children begin absorbing myths at an early age. Think about how they are bombarded by messages and metaphors in music, television, and movies. I found these in Disney's smash hit *The Lion King*, but they show up in many Disney tales: Wisdom is weak; what you need for a leader is a powerful carnivore; the most intense lure is sex or revenge; physical force and guilt dominate intelligence; evil lies just beyond your border; don't let the herbivores vote; a lioness cannot lead.

Parents, of course, are the source of some of the most compelling myths. If our parents fear or disdain people who are different from them, we often grow up to fear or disdain them too. Myths and the stories associated with them usually demonize those we fear, and that perception becomes a part of a child's eventual character as an adult.

Myths are a conservative force. They sanctify the existing beliefs (secretaries are paid less than machinists, assault weapons are just rifles, females are better parents). American myths about physicians accord them the respect and control once extended to medicine men or mystics. Lawyers dominate politics because we equate legislative processes with legal procedures.

Myths change as cultures change—or as we become more familiar with what was once "strange" or "foreign." We are left to sort it all out according to "what feels right." But more often than not, what feels right is what we were once told was right, and we resist change even in the face of new information or new interpretations of events. Nevertheless, as cultures change, old myths are being challenged and new myths are being created. Knowing how myths—old and new—affect thought and behavior will improve your ability to make decisions based on reality. Added to an understanding of changing social trends and patterns, myth awareness will enhance your ability to sense the future.

PLAY WITH MYTHS

In times of change, knowing what myths are losing power and what new myths are being created is important. Here are some universal myths that are now being challenged by social analysts. Do any of these affect your life or business?

> Physical battle makes a man strong
> Suffering makes a woman feminine
> Sexual access is a reward for courage or power
> The hero submits to and is guided by a higher power
> Animals don't feel pain
> Babies don't have memories
> The world is dualistic; if one group moves up the
>   other must move down
> God is on our side
> Justice for all
> Leaders must be strong and willful
> Western civilization is the best civilization
> Secrecy is power

SYMBOLS

A symbol, such as the menorah or the cross, is a summary of the myths it represents. It is an outward sign of an inward belief. A true symbol does more than just represent something else. It also generates an awareness of the beliefs, promises, or myths behind the symbol. A powerful symbol may be the best argument in many debates. That is why prolife demonstrators display fetuses. We have social symbols (clothes, language) and business symbols (the executive suite, company logos) that represent who we are. We have sign symbols to identify public toilets and tell us when to stop our cars. Nations also have important symbols. The American flag unites us and reminds us of our identity; thus the intense feelings that are aroused when the American flag is desecrated. The British long resisted the Chunnel because the English Channel symbolizes their proud image as an island kingdom, separate from Europe. The underwater Chunnel dashes that image. The cross instantly evokes the beliefs and emotions of Christianity. When Madonna played with a crucifix onstage, she stirred many layers of myth.

Language is dense with symbols. It is difficult to carry a thought in your head, let alone pass it on, without some way to symbolize it. The words you choose are often symbols that reveal who you are and what you believe. When techies call managers "manglers" and bodybuilders call weaker men "wimps," these words symbolize what is being thought.

Language and its symbols change constantly as our beliefs and our perceptions change and we seek new ways to express them. The proliferation of politically correct terms such as "physically challenged" and "visually impaired" is an example. There will always be clumsy extremes. But this language is inspired by the belief that words must be used in a sensitive manner when describing our fellow human beings. The "n" word became a symbol of police corruption in the O. J. Simpson trial. Words, after all, let you do things to people. "Savages" can be killed, "Native Americans" cannot. "Girls" can be trifled with, "women" cannot. "Cripples, morons, and defectives" can be scorned, "people with disabilities" cannot.

When you use terms that indicate respect for people rather than dehumanizing them, it alters your perception of how you should treat them. Companies especially are paying attention to this fact. They cannot hope to manage a diverse workforce or develop a diverse clientele in a global market if they fail to speak of people with respect. Language is the public relations tool of the mind; it reveals your consciousness.

Language has always changed or you would be speaking "olde English" now. When you notice that word usage is changing, see if you can detect the change in symbolism, too. When the term "bastard" began to apply to everyone instead of just an illegitimate child, it was a signal that single parenting was becoming acceptable. When computer "nerds" became "hackers" or "techies," their image was also changing. As computer users become mainstream, the pejorative labels will disappear or be applied to the technically impaired.

MYTHS, SYMBOLS, AND BUSINESS

Corporate myths are based on tradition, preferences, prejudice, or stereotypes. They are passed on from one generation of managers and workers to the next, often in the form of stories or legends about events and people in the company's history. Few of those inside an organization are conscious of the process. But such myths invariably limit management's vision.

Sometimes, a company seems to cling to old myths and symbols that can be sold to its executives and workers but not to younger consumers. The "your true voice" ad campaign of AT&T struck me that way. The slogan translated as "We're the 'real' telephone company," but that is no longer true. It may work as an illusion or myth for consumers over fifty but not for Generation X.

Leadership styles in companies are heavily influenced by myth. Give executives a list of the heroes of their youth and ask them which ones resonate. Some mention movie cowboys—John Wayne and Gary Cooper score well. Others cite sports figures—it's no surprise that the two top business motivational speakers in 1994 were Pat Riley and Jimmy Johnson, both coaches.

But the hands-down favorite in these surveys is the Lone Ranger. The concepts surrounding this myth are powerful: Work alone, except for a trusted semiservant who has no real status. Don't tell people what you are doing. Disguise yourself. Have no personal life. Ride a flashy horse. Believe you are exceptional, a crusader. The ideal is of a strong, moral man bringing security to others and asking nothing in return except total control. We are all attracted to a hero, a father, a champion who will fight for us. It is the universal myth of a god disguised as a stranger who comes to the rescue.

Imagine the Lone Ranger running your company; perhaps he does. He is not a communicator. He rides into town, does what has to be done, and rides out. The townspeople have to guess who he is, refrain from asking questions, and assume he is doing the right thing. This guy is not a team player. He is expensive; you can imagine the maintenance on the white horse and the cost of silver bullets. He wears a mask because he has not solved any of his past personal problems, and we have no idea what he is doing with Tonto. The Spanish word *tonto* means "stupid."

Corporate symbols include everything from the company logo to the outfits employees wear. They tell the workers—and the outside world—a great deal about an organization. Exxon, when it was paying damages to fishermen after the *Valdez* oil spill, rented offices in Seattle. It also leased black Lincoln Continentals and parked them in a row in front of the entrance to its claims center. I watched arriving fishermen walk past those cars and mentally add a zero to their claims. Exxon either did not care or was unaware that it was creating an impression of "big bad oil."

IBM failed to appreciate what the uniformity of its white-shirted service representatives said about the company. Engineers at Boeing, an IBM client, once complained to me, "We want a cutting-edge consultant, you know, a guy with an earring, a little weird. Not someone who looks just like us and only knows what we know."

One large information-services company I work with has a multimillion-dollar conference center, built ten years ago to be "state-of-the-art." It conveys in dramatic terms the vision of the previous CEO and the fortunes of the company. The place is beige, heavy, quiet, low-energy, controlled, like a mausoleum. The conference rooms have no windows, the chairs are bolted to the floors, and the evening dining arrangements are formal. The guest rooms are like upholstered monastic chambers.

On my first visit, the corporate culture that this place symbolized gave off such a strong odor of death that I sold my stock as soon as I got to my cell and could pick up a telephone. The stock plunged for almost two years, until another CEO took over. He will have to sell the conference center. It would make a good home for a religious order.

In fact, more than one corporate headquarters has been sold (Sears, IBM, Citibank, CBS), not only as a cost-saving measure but also as recognition that what the building symbolized had become irrelevant. Huge monuments to corporate culture were built in the early 1980s, just before that culture began to collapse. We were lucky the Japanese bought some of them.

The composition of a workforce can also be an important symbol. When I spoke to a group of four hundred managers at a Martin Marietta plant, I was surprised that there were no minorities and only one woman, a visiting engineer from Holland, in the audience. The symbolism of a virtually all-white, male room in the 1990s, and what that suggested about the company, was powerful.

In some organizations, this kind of symbolism is more covert. The Army Corps of Engineers, the CIA, and American oil companies are good examples. I saw posters on the walls promoting a respectful work environment, but the informal messages these organizations were giving to their people were quite the opposite—and far more potent. Women, and men thought to be weak or different, were called insulting names. Offensive physical gestures were common in the offices. One corporate officer had an open affair with a subordinate. People were regularly threatened if they complained. But when I mentioned this behavior to a manager, he said he couldn't imagine what I was talking about. I was facing the not-to-be-questioned power of the past.

Albert J. Dunlap, who has developed a reputation as a turnaround specialist, keeps an ornament on his desk of circling sharks. "You must get rid of the people who represent the old culture, or they will fight you," he says. "And you have to get rid of all the old symbols." If old symbols stay in place, too many people assume that nothing has changed and that they need only wait out the newcomers.

When it comes to preserving myths, the navy is hard to beat. It has maintained a rigid, sealed culture because of the beliefs of top-ranking officers that they are "chosen" and can, in turn, choose to exclude others—women and minorities, in particular. Even with ongoing reform, their myths guarantee them many more embarrassments and lawsuits. The army, however, has been transformed; its practices provide us with a glimpse of the future.

Army leaders apparently realized in 1973 that without the draft they had to provide real incentives for enlistment. Thus, its leadership training was overhauled to focus on adaptive management, flexibility, international citizenship, self-esteem, teamwork, ethics, and zero tolerance for racism. In the process, the army became a model learning organization. Many personnel directors tell me they would rather hire a new employee with four years of army training than one with four years of college. The army, they maintain, teaches its recruits the skills that work with diverse, egalitarian, technically competent, empowered teams.

When an organization embarks on change, it must create new myths and symbols for its people. Some companies encourage change by bringing in outsiders. Canon hires middle managers from outside the company. Honda does the same, and looks especially for those who it believes will bring in new ideas. Others, like Pepsi, rotate their best people between field office, home office, marketing, distribution, and product development to break up subcultures.

NOTICING THE CHANGES

Old symbols and myths are often threatened or uprooted without our realizing it at the time. The passion that surrounds such moments makes it difficult to recognize that change is in the air, as was demonstrated by the Senate hearings on the confirmation of Clarence Thomas's appointment to the Supreme Court, during which Anita Hill testified that he had sexually harassed her. The male tribal elders on the committee were confronted with so many myths they were dizzy: black men as sex machines, scorned women as liars, white men lynching black men, and so on. Symbolic ground was broken over and over again. An educated, articulate African-American woman discussed penises and pubic hairs on national television. The senators asked her to repeat the details over and over again as if they could not comprehend what she was saying.

The chairman, Joseph Biden, could not understand the power of the myths he was refereeing, and this frightened him into avoidance. Colleagues Arlen Spector, Alan Simpson, and Orrin Hatch were apoplectic as they saw the old code collapsing, not because they were mean men but because they were rigid. They were willing to break judicial rules and resort to slander to prevent the crumbling of their beliefs about the behavior and motivations of men and women. Senator Ted Kennedy wisely kept quiet.

An individual who holds on to the old symbols and myths after they have lost their relevance can be an embarrassment. An obvious example is the old-style coach who insults and manhandles players, using humiliation as a weapon. These coaches create the life-and-death battles of tribal warfare and cause their players to act accordingly. But the myth of games as warfare has lost its relevance. New-style coaches motivate their players through strategy, teamwork, inspiration, and confidence. They teach their players to think and work together.

Corporations used to hire tough-coach types as managers and salesmen, and told employees to obey them without question. Many have now retired or been fired. They may be legends in their companies—but not legends that any sensible business leader would want to emulate. They have become a part of an old corporate myth, symbols of the past. But their examples remind us that corporate myths do change and employees need to know this. When workers hear too many stories of "the way things used to be," the message is that the company wants to relive the past. Employees need to hear stories of the future, how things are *going* to be. That's the "vision thing."

Corporate symbols are useful indicators of whether

change is taking place. The allocation of corporate space, always symbolically important, is an example. There is no way to encourage empowerment if the parking lots, offices, and lunchrooms are still allocated on the basis of hierarchy and rank. In fact, the shape and feel of a building alone can reveal whether you are dealing with a 1950s management style or a 1990s one. Does it get quieter as you walk toward the executive offices? Is there a clash between a company's stated willingness to change and what it actually does to encourage change? Company executives are often the most resistant to change, the least able to tolerate the loss of status or control.

When a symbol changes it almost always indicates that something of real substance is also changing. The Vietnam War memorial is a powerful public example. This monument, unsettling to many when it was first unveiled, symbolizes a dramatic shift in America's myths about war. The war dead are no longer anonymous; they are named as individuals. Instead of a tribute to victory, the memorial is a list of touchable names carved in granite that mirrors our own troubled reflections. Now the most important criterion for American engagement in combat seems to be the potential loss of American lives.

We might expect leaders to be the first to recognize that beliefs, as well as the myths that reinforce them, have changed. In Italy, the myth of the Mafia as legendary heroes protecting their own code of honor vanished with the realization that it is an organization of thugs and extortionists that hurts everyone. But Premier Giulio Andreotti missed seeing that change and was indicted in the backlash. Presidential candidate Bill Clinton should have just said that he inhaled—the myths around marijuana had already changed. Prince Charles seemed surprised when his extramarital dalliance with Camilla Parker-Bowles was so roundly condemned. He had overlooked the British public's growing distaste for sexual hypocrisy.

Companies that know when myths and beliefs are

changing can respond with marketing images that are in sync with the changes. The creative advertising firm of Bartle, Bogle, Hegarty, for example, dropped sexual images for simplicity and soul in its ads for Levi's; ads for Calvin Klein did not. Recycling and other environmental themes have become selling points for Shell, Weyerhauser, Waste Management, and other natural-resource-based corporations. Samsung ads talk about preserving "our ecosphere." The planet is featured in far more ads now than the outline of a particular state or country.

Changing myths and beliefs can also have profound product implications. But some companies don't pick up on the signals until competitors take over their markets. Detroit automakers lost out to Japanese manufacturers in the 1970s because beliefs about quality, reliability, fuel efficiency, and cost had changed. Myths about the inferiority of anything "made in Japan" had also changed. Patriotism was no longer powerful enough to stop the purchase of foreign goods in an increasingly global marketplace, although American companies tried to fight back with "buy America" campaigns—and still do.

MYTHS AND SYMBOLS
IN THE GLOBAL VILLAGE

The play *Six Degrees of Separation* was based on the idea that "we are all connected," the notion that you need to know only six people to have a connection with everyone on earth, even someone as distant as a Kalahari Bushman. This "new myth" of global intimacy, however philosophical, is already taking shape. Ted Turner's vision and the creation of CNN multiplied our shared news, our shared heroes and heroines, and put us all at the same table. We are in McLuhan's "global embrace."

When different cultures meet, myths and beliefs begin to mingle. Women in China are taking off their revolutionary suits and putting on American styles. The Russian evening news is televised in the United States on C-SPAN. The Bobbitts and O. J. Simpson were given almost as much media attention in Japan as they were here. The tabloid press is international. We shrink the planet further when we can discuss and gossip about the same events and people.

Teenagers around the world increasingly wear the same kinds of clothes, eat the same kinds of food, read the same publications, listen to the same music, and watch the same television programs. The lucrative international trade in classic Levi's tells us that the independent American cowboy is a myth, and an image, that many of the world's teenagers are adopting.

American mass culture remains the great experiment, all things to all people, choose what you want. So it is not surprising that our myths and beliefs are dominant, made so in large part by our media powerhouse. Eighty-eight of the world's hundred most-attended films in 1994 were American. *L.A. Law* and *Major Dad* were big in South Africa; Whitney Houston and *The Bold and the Beautiful* were hits in Egypt. The PBS special on the Civil War aired three times in Germany, while Poland watched reruns of *Dallas* and *The Bill Cosby Show*. Linda Evans of *Dynasty* fame was stunned on a trip to India to find villagers who recognized her as Crystal.

Some cultures try to protect themselves from this kind of "cultural pollution," but with relatively little success. But American companies that are players in the global economy have to tread carefully. They need to examine the beliefs they hold of their overseas clients or customers, as well as the images they and their products convey. Above all, they need to be aware of the myths and beliefs of the people of every country and culture where their goods or services are sold.

The Disney experience is an instructive one. Its ambivalence about translating American pop culture into Japan and France led the company to make a double mistake. It didn't retain a financial interest in Tokyo's Disneyland and it held on to a substantial interest in Euro Disney in France. The result: It suffered an initial loss of more than a billion dollars in France and it cut itself out of millions of dollars of profit in the most successful Disneyland of all—the one in Japan. These two different outcomes remind us that a culture's myths about itself are always very powerful. Business leaders who fail to take these myths into account are risking failure.

After World War II, when Japan set out to rebuild itself, the nation saw America as its model of success and affluence. The Japanese taught their children English and learned everything they could from their American occupiers. As soon as they could afford it, they came to the United States in droves as tourists. At home, the younger generation idolized Elvis, sang country-western songs in karaoke bars, loved baseball, and made McDonald's the largest fast-food chain in Tokyo. In their recreation the Japanese seemed to love anything "pop," and they loved clean. The Disney ethic of sanitized fantasy experiences fit the bill perfectly. Further, it could exist side-by-side with still strongly held cultural beliefs. There was no conflict.

Contrast that with the belief of the French that theirs is *the* culture and that any other culture poses a threat. They refused to teach English in their schools long after it became the language of commerce. They enacted laws to prevent the use of foreign words such as *cheeseburger* and *software*, and have tried to legislate controls on the distribution of American films and television programs. They claim our fast food is abominable, and they do not want a sanitized recreational experience. They like a little more passion and sleaze—a richer, sexier, more sophisticated fantasy world. Furthermore, they have *real* castles and ancient villages, and a long history of great achievements in art, architecture, and music. Whereas the Japanese can adapt to cultural change because they sense it is superficial, the French resist cultural change because they fear that new myths could supplant the old. French ethnocentrism is so intense (consider the French-speaking province of Quebec's recent attempt to secede from Canada) that it overrides most other considerations.

Ethnocentric myths can cause all sorts of businesses to stumble. Turner Broadcasting executives, however, were sensitized to cultural differences from Day One. They knew, for example, that Porky Pig cartoons might offend Muslims, who abstain from eating pork because they believe it to be unclean. TBS dropped Porky from the cartoon programs it sends to Indonesia and other Muslim nations. Farsighted businesses will learn to read the symbols of the myths that will endure and of those in the process of change.

MYTH SWITCHES

Business leaders also need to develop the ability to recognize myth switches and sort out those that are important because they announce changes in our culture. The film *Dances with Wolves* turned old beliefs upside down. It was a reversal for adults raised on classic westerns. Native Americans were once portrayed as savages who were dirty, ignorant, heathen—and, anyway, we wanted their land. Now we are taught that Native Americans were spiritual, in balance with the environment, had strong family ties, and, the low blow, were better lovers. General Custer isn't a hero anymore; he is a thug.

Recent events at The Citadel can serve as a classic example of myth switching. What happened when a young woman sought to gain admission to that all-male academy in fall 1995 was much more than an attempt at gender integration. It was an assault on all the old myths that promised The Citadel's young male graduates a place in the military or the corporate South: a code of silence, loss of individuality, situational ethics, class restrictions, punishment for any diversion from the company line, male domination, and absolute loyalty. These myths were taught in an environment that allowed students to be harassed, beaten, and humiliated into submission.

Can leaders still develop in a *Lord of the Flies*, "survival of the fittest" atmosphere? The belief that equates toughness and loyalty with humiliation is ancient. Gangs on the streets of Los Angeles practice it, as have all warrior societies. The deeper question raised by The Citadel dispute is not what myths and symbols will change, but what truly serves a quality workforce and the world we live in and what does not.

High school administrators are also struggling with redefining leadership education. Many want to eliminate football because it is a hunting-and-gathering ritual, a band of men chasing a pig, with cheerleaders (the fertile females) as the ultimate reward. Teachers tell me they support "reduced sport schools" because they cannot inspire the knowledge worker of the future if he or she has to walk through halls being humiliated by the heroes of the past.

Another myth switch reveals the ambivalence that always accompanies change. There are frequently lines outside women's toilets at meetings and public gatherings, but seldom outside men's toilets. There have been reports of women being arrested for using male facilities at concerts. Now, legislatures are being forced to add "potty parity" to their design codes. What is going on here?

Toilet facilities for women were not a major consideration in the days when they worked at home, attended public events in fewer numbers, and, when pregnant, were sequestered. When all that changed, the lines started to form. Women, it turned out, needed more time and more privacy to use toilets than men. Architects tried to speed things up by removing the bathroom counters, so women had no place to put their purses and packages. It seemed logical from a male point of view. Then the coat hooks began to disappear. Women responded by stacking their coats on the trash cans, but new rounded domes added on top of the cans ended that. So the lines kept increasing as women appeared in the outside world in greater numbers and tried to keep their purses, packages, and children off rest room floors. It took years before anyone began making reasonable attempts to review and solve the problem.

The great toilet dilemma is a reminder that even experts often take a long time to recognize the obvious— that something of substance has changed. In this case, it was the new participation of women in events outside the home. A business that is able to detect such a shift in its early stages can offer services or products ahead of the crowd. When architects and designers became more aware of the problem, some new convention centers featured rest rooms with partitions that can be easily moved to reapportion the space allotted to both sexes, depending on who is attending the conference and how long the lines are. Each rest room has a door for men at one end, a door for women at the other end, and a movable wall in between.

The new convention center in Portland, Oregon, presents an eye-catching example of our toilet malevolence. The stalls in the women's toilet have, baked into the tiles just in front of each commode, the image of a spider. The unwary woman sits down, only to jump up. The men's toilet has, baked into approximately the same floor tiles, the image of a waterfall.

MYTH AND SYMBOL SKILLS

In times of rapid transition, individuals who can recognize myth shifts will stay well ahead of the pack. But this requires the ability to relax the barriers we usually erect when encountering something new. We have to shed the inhibitions placed on our thinking by age, gender, experience, and training.

We can untangle the truth behind symbols and myths if we can get at what they really represent. One way is to ask questions of ourselves. What beliefs supported the use of tobacco or the actions that promote environmental degradation? Is it an illusion that cigarettes are sexy or that we need to develop coastal oil reserves? Does the historical rationale still fit the belief that Native Americans are savages or that woman's place is in the home? Was it good for the company, and for how long, to think that customer service wasn't important or that we can control the infrastructure?

Here are some other ways to expand our awareness of changing myths and symbols.

Check Out Children's Myths

Most adults are only dimly aware of, or actively resist, the changing myths of the next generation. They prefer their own, and so they take their children to see *Snow White, The Little Mermaid,* and *Beauty and the Beast.* But if they think the fairy tales of their youth are superior to the stories that today's children select, they should consider the following: Snow White's family is dysfunctional, with a stepmother plotting murder and an absent father. Snow White runs away and ends up housekeeping for seven bachelors who have disturbing personal habits. Is this what you want for your daughter? Snow lacks assertiveness, ends up in a coma, and the only way out is the kiss of a prince. No one suggests she get an education.

The Little Mermaid gives up her greatest talent, her voice, in order to pay for major plastic surgery, so she can have feet and the prince. Have you checked out the quality of princes lately? They are not what they used to be.

Japanese Crown Prince Naruhito had to propose many times, and many women wondered why Masako Owada said yes.

On one level, *Beauty and the Beast* tells us to love others regardless of their physical appearance. But the real message is that the love of a good woman still can eliminate the beast in any man. Check out the statistics on spousal abuse.

On the other hand, children have the Teenage Mutant Ninja Turtles, a new fairy tale for a new generation. The heroes begin life as pet store turtles that a child is carrying in a jar of water. The child trips, and the turtles fall into the New York sewer system, where they are drenched by a radioactive spill. They mutate into Ninja warriors with the skills of both East and West. They are named Michelangelo, Leonardo, Raphael, and Donatello (after Renaissance artists). They spend their days combating crime and violence while living in the underbelly of New York.

Children are fascinated by power struggles, the good guys versus the bad guys, so they are drawn to models of combat. But not many kids play cowboys and Indians or cops and robbers anymore. The new battles are more complex. The Ninja Turtles fight with the tools of the martial arts—they do not use guns or knives; they do not draw blood. The turtles work as a team, despite their different personalities. They also know how to have fun, and their favorite food is pizza with sushi on it. Splinter, a sewer rat who is a Zen master, is their revered spiritual guide. He teaches the turtles all the future skills: discipline, higher forms of consciousness and communication, mediation and meditation, teamwork, stress reduction, and ethics.

The Ninja Turtles combined old and new, and even cross-cultural, symbols in a way that hit a new generation as just right. The Mighty Morphin Power Rangers, the latest craze, are a multiethnic team of boys *and* girls who fight evil by transforming themselves into cyborgs

with incredible "techie" powers. Having an awareness of
the next generation's myths and models will help you
keep track of new realities. The next time your kids
pester you to buy a Ninja Turtle or a Power Ranger, ask
yourself why. What messages do these images really convey? We all know what myths and messages G.I. Joes
and Barbie dolls convey.

Watch or Read Science Fiction

The thrills and excitement of science fiction are irre-
sistible for many people. But the real power of science
fiction may be in the new myths and new social relations
that are found in it—for example, in the various *Star Trek*
TV series. Taken together, these shows have had strong
pop culture influences on all those who have grown up
with them. The themes—human anxieties and quests—
are familiar, but they are brought to life by a new breed
of heroes and heroines whose spacecraft is a shining example of a positive future. The starship *Enterprise* is a self-
contained world in which instant communication and
information are available. Its mission, "to go where no
one has gone before," is inspirational. Crew members are
self-reliant and highly ethical. Their explorations are
guided by the Prime Directive: No one may interfere
with the normal development of any society.

Young adults especially like Captain Jean Luc Picard,
whose most familiar response to input from the bridge
crew is "Make it so!" Picard is a unique executive model.
He is small in stature and uses both consensus and his
own intuition to make decisions. He plays the flute, tends
an aquarium, reads poetry and classic myths, and fences
for physical exercise. But he keeps a western saddle in
his closet just in case he lands on a planet that has horses.

Each of the technologies used on the starship has a
basis in our known reality. Voice commands are used. A
request to find a location on the ship is given to a wall
that lights up and shows the way. "Turbolifts" act as ele-

vators but can move sideways as well as up and down. Oxygen is generated by cryogenic fluid transfer. Technology is liberating.

In George Orwell's *1984*, technology strips man of freedom. Jules Verne's *20,000 Leagues Under the Sea* pictures the exploration of new worlds as filled with terrible dangers. Most older science fiction focused on imagined technology more than human psychology, relationships, or diversity. Current science fiction is far more positive, particularly in its portrayals of a multicultural universe of citizens able to balance the technical and personal advances of their time. Compare the terrifying space aliens of the past to the lovable E.T.—another myth switch.

Survey the Arts

Ezra Pound wrote: "The artist is the antennae of the race." Art provides many of our symbols and therefore clues to the future. Artists usually are the first to break with a declining style and establish a new form. Their imaginations can be an early-warning system of what is in the air, radar that looks into the psyche of a society.

The work of Norman Rockwell, perhaps America's most famous illustrator, was often featured on the covers of national magazines. But he frequently challenged the status quo. In 1961, a cover for *The Saturday Evening Post* showed the diverse people of the world captioned with the phrase "Do unto others as you would have them do unto you." That same idea was later used in the "I'd like to give the world a Coke" television ad, which featured children from all over the world holding hands.

One of Rockwell's most famous paintings shows a little African-American girl in a puff-sleeve dress being escorted toward a school door by four huge U.S. marshals while angry whites jeer and throw tomatoes. He titled it "The Problem We All Live With," and *Look* published it in early 1964. The Civil Rights Act passed six months later.

Many futurists are predicting a renaissance in literature and the arts as we create new myths for the twenty-first century. This trend is already noticeable in crowded bookstores and art galleries. More people go to museums and the theater than attend sports events in New York and other major cities. If Impressionism in the late 1800s and Expressionism in the 1950s reconfigured our perceptions of reality, what art will reconfigure it in the year 2000?

Watch for New Symbols

Old ways, even those easily proven to be impractical or irrational, seem impossible to change (for example, drunk driving, tobacco use, environmental pollution, waste of water resources). But then along come new symbols that people can readily connect to and change is suddenly in the air. In the Northwest, the plight of the spotted owl was not enough to inspire most citizens to demand protection of old-growth timber. The threatened loss of jobs was too upsetting. But the potential loss of Coho salmon was another matter entirely. Few men had seen the owl, but many had thrilled to salmon on their lines. Children had seen the salmon leaping up fish ladders at dam sites, played with fingerlings at hatcheries, and worn the Coho image on caps and T-shirts. Salmon were a symbol of the abundance of the Northwest; to lose them would be to lose the dream. Citizens rallied behind the salmon. Sometimes, the right symbols will accomplish what scientific data cannot.

Lung cancer was not immediate enough to inspire inquiries into tobacco industry ethics, but secondhand smoke was. Killing convenience store clerks or gang members didn't add much momentum to gun-control efforts, but killing children, tourists, and visiting students did. The death of a celebrity has an impact far beyond the many deaths of unknowns. Rock Hudson's death from AIDS and Magic Johnson's retirement from and return to professional basketball after he discovered he was HIV positive are examples. When the audience can personalize the victim, beliefs change.

Survey Advertising

When advertising metaphors shift noticeably (from sports to the creative arts, for example), it can be a tip-off to changing times. Gap advertising tried to broaden the appeal of its khaki products with ads featuring Andy Warhol, Miles Davis, Allen Ginsberg, Steve McQueen, and Zsa Zsa Gabor. *Forbes* magazine ran an ad campaign featuring younger, entrepreneurial corporate chieftains like Craig McCaw of McCaw Cellular and Scott F. McNealy of Sun Microsystems Inc. rather than older, more traditional CEOs. Bartle, Bogle, Hegarty nostalgia ads for Levi-Strauss used themes of American opportunity, freedom, sex, and rebellion worldwide. A new pop-culture drink from Coke, OK, was aimed at skeptical or weary teenage boys.

Watch the "Other" Channels

John Leland, writing in *Newsweek*, described MTV's production center as a "Marshall McLuhan rec room, a place where precociously creative young people invent cool ways to frame ugly heavy-metal videos." European teenagers learn American English skills by watching MTV. New clothing styles such as hip-hop move directly from MTV to store racks. An MTV shopping network cannot be far away.

The Discovery Channel includes programs on how things work. One show, *The Secret Life of Machines*, takes the mystery out of new technology but preserves the magic. Other programs run the gamut from software instruction to dream analysis. Discovery is a contemporary *National Geographic*.

CNN was only briefly the "other" network; now it is *the* network for news and information. CNN sets a model for nonstar anchors, truly international correspondents, and a variety of world viewpoints. C-SPAN shows Senate debates and other such proceedings in their entirety, giving viewers a firsthand look. ITN (International Television News) provides world perspectives from outside the United States. All of these channels are indicators of changing realities and our perceptions of them.

Check the Sitcom Trends

Roseanne is everything women have denied they were free to be. She has no tolerance for the pretenses of a Mary Richards in *The Mary Tyler Moore Show*. She is prescient, talented, strong, funny, loud, opinionated, rudely honest, and fat. There is very little separation between Roseanne in real life and what you see on television. *Roseanne* represents the "opposite model," a key element in a myth switch. Yet she is in sync with Americans on most social issues. After beautifying her appearance, she is still a working-class everywoman—but with the plastic surgery and liposuction that many women of fortysomething, regardless of class, desire.

Ellen, Seinfeld, and Friends are "reality" sitcoms about how to navigate the complexities of single life. *Mad About You* and *Home Improvement* do the same with marriage. These close-to-real-life relationship struggles, regardless of whose they are, have become more interesting than those of the fantasy rich or perfect. Reality sitcoms are reflections of what is becoming more important in our lives. Try to create the next sitcom in your mind. Look around you at the new realities. What do you want help with or help laughing at? I'm calling mine *Flaccid Pines;* it's a sitcom set in a spa in Montana for middle-aged men and women in transition.

Notice the Best-sellers

The best-seller lists are always sending us messages. The popularity of books by physicists and scientists, for example, may be a sign of how eager we are to understand our universe. More books are being published on evolution (*The Moral Animal*) and primates (*Ishmael*). Spiritual best-sellers (*The Celestine Prophecy, The Road Less Traveled, Care of the Soul*) are read by people trying to find meaning in this new world. Books on death and near-death experiences do well as the baby-boomers create myths for their exit. The "hippie" child whose mother was a clairvoyant and whose father was a contortionist is depressed because he can see his own end. Health and health-care books are popular for somewhat the same reason: Our population is aging.

Notice Children's Books

One children's book publisher, Golden Books, now offers alternative versions of classic fairy tales. You can buy a nonviolent *Three Little Pigs* (no boiling of the wolf) or a modern *Little Red Riding Hood* (advising that you don't talk to strangers). New stories for kids are far more environmentalist, egalitarian, racially sensitive, and holistic than those of only a decade ago. They are also more realistic, and the young reader learns about, among many other real-life situations, conflict resolution and divorce.

Notice New Magazines

A successful new magazine identifies a niche and the growth trends of that niche. Scan the magazine racks for the latest additions. You may be surprised at how specialized they are. If you are a business executive, you might want to weigh the advertising possibilities. My favorite is *Wired*.

   Out is a national magazine aimed at affluent gay men and lesbians. Its circulation doubled within the first two years to more than 100,000. Advertisers have included Absolut vodka, Benetton clothes, Geffen records, Banana Republic, Sony Electronics, Apple Computer, and American Express. Time Inc. Ventures is considering its own publication for gays.

PC, Windows, Mobile Office, Home Office, and *Wired* are hot sellers. Other niche magazines include *Internet World, P.C. Novice, Home Defense, Handgunner, Trailer Life, Black Beat, Sport Truck, Safe and Secure Living, Muscle Magazine, Fitness Plus, Cigar Aficionado, In-Fisherman, Vegetarian Times, Fast & Healthy, Mouth 2 Mouth, Bone Bug Journal* (for fossil hunters), and *Edge.*

Prisoners are no longer viewed as destitute. *Prison Life* taps a $2 billion captive market—the average prisoner spends $1,200 to $1,500 a year at the prison commissary. The cover story in one issue of *Prison Life,* titled "Tough Guys Open Up," describes men's support groups behind the walls. Advertisers offer audiotapes, bodybuilding products, electric massagers, running shoes, and harmonicas. Lawyers advertise their services. Tobacco advertisements are welcome. The biggest sellers in the commissaries: Hostess cupcakes, Pepsi, and cigarettes.

Pick Up on Anomalies, Opposites, and Tension

There is creative tension in opposites. Philosopher John Beckett calls it "sandpaper on the brain." Myths and symbols often represent extremes: life/death, good/evil, male/female, power/weakness, love/hate, peace/war, light/dark. Change always requires us to modify the pull between such opposites. But we are beginning to understand and accept that in many cases it is no longer either/or but both—or something in between.

When we are unable to resolve opposites, the old myths fall apart. Anomalies arise that confuse and limit us. Executives demand innovation but punish mistakes. Voters demand change but simultaneously resist it. The public expresses a fear of violence but watches increasingly violent sports and media. Notice opposites or anomalies and try to predict their resolutions. They often signal new trends.

Watch Trends in Other Countries

Other countries struggle with their myths just as we do. Knowing about their experiences broadens our perspective on change and what may lie ahead. In Egypt, for example, female genital mutilation is an age-old practice surrounded by mythology. When government officials agreed in 1995 to allow the procedure to be done in clinics and hospitals, it was an indication of the myth's amazing power. The government frowns on the practice, but saw no other way to prevent little girls from dying on the tables of private practitioners.

Saudi Arabia does not allow women to drive cars even though many are university-educated professionals. Myths about the place of women in that society prevail over their desire for freedom and independence. The women resist by wearing jeans and American T-shirts under the flowing black chadors that must cover their bodies. The conflict between old and new becomes surreal when female Muslim athletes wear Gor-Tex chadors to compete in Olympic events.

India is wrestling with both gender and class changes. The Bandit Queen, Phoolan Devi, has already achieved legendary status there. Also known as the Avenging Angel, she is changing the perception of what it means to be a woman and an untouchable in India. Devi, a fisherman's daughter, was sold at the age of eleven to an older man for a cow. She escaped, was taken captive by a gang, and was repeatedly raped. Later, she organized her own robber band to protest lower-caste misery and male repression. Released recently after eleven years in prison, Devi now wears a saffron sari and is a political figure. Dolls of her carrying a gun are sold across India. She is a new symbol of the global fraying of class societies.

Death Rattles

When old myths and symbols no longer serve us, they must be abandoned. But be prepared for them to die a messy death. They go down fighting; you can hear their "death rattles." Organizations caught in this situation often fail to recognize what is happening. Their leaders adopt rigid positions and engage in moral diatribes, sometimes resisting until the organization is decimated. The death rattles keep sounding, but it is very hard to let go of the old reliables.

Physical size is an interesting example of this. It is an ancient myth that largeness signifies power and status. It will lose its dominance in the modern workplace as we become knowledge workers, but it is still influential. Most executives, politicians, and leaders are still taller or bigger than average. Taller men are more likely to be hired, receive higher starting salaries, and get promoted more often than shorter men. The taller candidate in presidential elections during this century has won 80 percent of the time. Studies show that we tend to believe individuals of high status are taller than they actually are.

Models of human size are replicated in many of our ideas of big business as equated with security or dominance. I once tried, as an experiment, to persuade high school girls to shift their romantic attentions to smaller boys. I pointed out that they might be especially well prepared for the new world, techies who were strategic thinkers with good communication and negotiation skills. How else would they have successfully survived junior high? The new lean-and-mean business strategy might be better described as small and "wired"; rightsizing has many implications. But hunters and gatherers respected silence and bulk. So did the high school girls, who told me they feel safer and sexier standing next to a guy who is bigger than they are.

New myths, symbols, and images take time to sort out if your responses to them are emotional. If those responses are unrelated to new realities, they will have an adverse effect on your life and your business. An awareness of the most powerful myths we believe in and act upon is a crucial leadership tool. Equally important is the ability to let go of those myths that no longer serve us. New myths and images signal changing realities. To stay abreast of change, you must be able to see what is going as well as what is coming. Look around you, look within, and check your own myths.

Speeding Up Your Response Time

"There are too many complaints about society having to move too fast to keep up with the machine. There is great advantage in moving fast if you move completely, if social, educational, and recreational changes keep pace."

—MARGARET MEAD,
QUOTED IN *TIME*, SEPTEMBER 4, 1954

CHANGE, EVEN IF PREDICTABLE, is almost always perceived as threatening. Even small changes are sources of tension. When I began teaching myself to use a computer twenty years ago, I put a kitchen timer nearby and set it to go off at fifteen-minute intervals. The idea was to hold down the panic. By keeping the lessons short in the beginning, I got past my resistance to learning something that required a plunge into the unknown. It also helped that I could actually measure my progress. Each time the printer spit out a document or I was able to find a file, I was a success.

Most change, however, doesn't come in such neatly defined segments; it seems constant and unrelenting. That makes it a bigger threat because there is no relief, no easy measure of success, no sense of closure—ever. Learning how to respond to and master the process of change—and even to excel at it—is a critical leadership skill for the twenty-first century. Constant, rapid change will be a fact of life for all of us.

I once spoke to a group of bankers after their CEO had assured them that, if they could just maintain their hectic pace for another quarter, things would slow down and get back to "normal." Banking had been stable for so long that change was still seen as an aberration. I had to break the news that the whirlwind speed of change their business was experiencing *was* normal. There wasn't a chance of anything slowing down. I could tell from the looks on their faces that many thought they couldn't keep up.

Most of us are not creatures of change. We came of age during times of relative economic stability. We saw our parents rewarded for their ability to endure, to stay in the same job or with the same company year after year. Happiness, we believed, was the automatic reward for a well-planned life. If we made a list of things to do, and followed it, we would at some point get to the end of the list and be able to relax and eventually retire. Life was predictable, a place for everything and everything in its place.

But then the thirty-somethings got caught in the competitive, fast-paced economy of the 1980s and the generation that followed found itself in a work world that was forever changing. Now we barely have time to get to the bottom of our lists before having to make—or being given—six other lists. The leatherbound personal organizers some people rely on have gotten so heavy they can no longer be carried. The sense of completion that we looked forward to experiencing is not there.

No wonder that the response of some people in the 1990s has been "burrowing," a full-scale retreat. They are intent on creating their own kind of comfort zone—the freezer full of food, the family room full of entertainment, and no need ever to go out again. Reactions like these are human nature. When change seems overwhelming, many people prefer the long-term dull ache that familiar problems of work or life can produce rather than risking the quick acute pain that the unknown can inflict.

THE PROCESSES OF CHANGE

Businesses and organizations are usually slow to respond to change. To speed up their response time, anyone in a leadership role should understand the traditional processes of change. Cultures and economies evolve over long periods of time in response to both internal and external change. Many industries and organizations do so as well. Here is a summary of the classic processes of cultural evolution:

- *Innovation*, or invention, is the discovery by a group or individual of a new practice, tool, or principle that eventually gains the acceptance of others (fire, the wheel, industrialization, cars, computers) and changes almost everything.
- *Diffusion* is cultural borrowing, the spread of cultural customs or practices (use of spices, the Westernization of Japan, democracy in Russia, total quality management).
- *Cultural loss* is experienced when something new and innovative displaces an older cultural trait, attribute, or practice (the loss of a language, the fading of class distinctions, the demise of a political system). At times, cultural loss will trigger resistance to change (as in male backlash, the attempted restoration of a monarchy, or top management's concentrating instead of diffusing its power).
- *Acculturation*, or assimilation, is the combining or blending of cultures. It results from intense first-hand contact with a previously "foreign" group (slaves brought to America from Africa, successive waves of European immigrants to the United States, Americans in Japan after World War II, the Japanese in Australia in the 1990s). But even after decades or centuries of contact, acculturation may still be superficial (ethnic and racial enclaves in large cities, gender ceilings in management).

- *Outside control* is the imposition of one culture upon another, often the legacy of colonialism or war. Such impositions are often deeply resented and bitterly fought. The tensions in the Middle East are the current example (the politics of oil, United Nations sanctions on Iraq, and the battles between Israelis and Palestinians). Economic necessities can also generate cultural change. The threat of trade wars and tariffs has pushed Japan closer to opening its markets to U.S. products.
- *Trade, travel,* and *communications* are facilitators of cultural change, speeding up all the other cultural change processes. When I was high in the Himalayas, I passed the open door of a small, dirt-floored hut and heard music. Inside, a Nepalese group was gathered around a battery-operated VCR with a Michael Jackson video on the screen. This place with no roads and no wires had access to electronic images and American culture. O. J. Simpson's ride on the San Diego Freeway, complete with police cars and helicopters, was witnessed, in real time, worldwide.

Just as cultures evolve, so do business organizations and their management styles. All the recent corporate strategies—pursuit of excellence, managing by walking around, reengineering, the learning organization, new organizational paradigms, flattened hierarchies—are marks of the evolutionary process. Can you list recent changes in the culture of your business or organization—in management-employee relationships, for example, or in customer service or computerization? How have these changes affected the working environment? How have they affected you personally? Take the time to examine your own evolution as a person. Trace your key motivators and beliefs to see how they have changed and why. Think about the differences among you, your parents, and your grandparents. How are your children different from you? Evaluate your own reactions. Have you been responsive or resistant to change?

TESTING YOUR FLEXIBILITY

The key to handling change is, of course, your ability to be flexible. As a test of your flexibility, try to incorporate change into your daily routine. Take an area of your life—a task you must perform each day, for example— and experiment with doing it differently. Here are some tests to help you assess your flexibility:

Everyday Situations

The CEO calls you in and says, "It's time for some changes around here."

What is your gut reaction? Do you brace yourself for trouble, even though you don't know what the supervisor has in mind? Sometimes your resistance is automatic: "Oh, no, I'm about to hear that we are going to downsize." Or do you feel a surge of optimism? "This might mean a new assignment or a promotion for me."

At dinner, your spouse or one of your children declares, "I think there are some things that need to change around this house."

What is your first response? Are you happy your spouse is such a flexible risk taker? Are you able to withhold immediate judgment? Or, like most of us, do you imagine the changes will be disruptive? When my son declared he had an announcement to make, my first thought was that he was about to tell us his girlfriend was pregnant. It turned out he was planning to cut his hair and return to college.

How would you react to the following? Give yourself a flexibility rating on a scale of 1 to 10.

Rigid 1 .... *10 Flexible*

- During a tightly scheduled day, someone makes a last-minute change in the time for a meeting that has been on your calendar for two weeks.
- Your company hires an efficiency expert to spend two weeks in your department.
- Your assistant returns from the barber with the hair on each side of his head cropped in the shape of lightning bolts.
- Your best customer decides to take a sabbatical and sail around the world.

Check how you talk to yourself and about yourself. Do any of the following phrases sound familiar?

"I'm the same as I've always been."
"It bothers me when plans change at the last minute."
"I don't like to make mistakes."
"I think things were better in the past."
"I am uncomfortable with these new people."

Don't grade yourself separately on your flexibility at home versus the workplace. You might be tempted to think, Well, I have to be strict at home but at work I need to appear more easygoing. In truth, there is usually not that much difference between our work personalities and our home personalities. If you are critical and overdemanding of your family, you are probably the same way at work. If you resist change in the workplace, you probably resist it at home. Your attitude toward change, your ability to be flexible, is rooted in your mind, whatever the setting.

The Vegetable Test

Believe it or not, your attitude toward vegetables can tell you something about your level of flexibility. Did you make your vegetable choices early in life and decide, for example, that lima beans would never cross your lips? Do you find it hard to imagine why *anybody* would like lima beans?

Most of us are willing to add another vegetable to our edible list occasionally, but we are cautious about it. When did you last add a new vegetable to your menu, and what was it? How long did it take you to concede that this previously rejected food had some merit? What is your attitude toward ethnic cuisines? Are you willing to explore? If not, why not?

Flexibility about vegetables may even be age-related. If you recently added broccoli to your list, you have just passed thirty-five. Brussels sprouts usually don't enter the picture until you pass forty, unless you are English. Eggplant is unique. If you were not raised in a family that served eggplant, you may add it to your diet only as the result of some other change in your life, such as falling in love with someone who likes to cook it.

If you are not open to some new tastes, you are probably resistant to change. After all, stretching your tongue is easier than stretching your mind. Assign yourself a new food a week. Try a new fruit, a new vegetable, a new juice, a new ice cream, a new sauce, or a new fish. Eat lunch in a different place or order a different entrée. Shop for groceries in a different store or pick up some ethnic fast food. Get a knowledgeable friend to take you for a new dining experience and explain to you, gently, what you are eating.

The Language Test

How easy is it for you to use new words? Can you understand *hard drive*, and are you comfortable saying "chair" instead of "chairman"? How often do you not know the meaning of a business term that everyone else seems to be using, such as *reengineering, paradigm shift,* or *synergy*? How flexible are you when it comes to learning new words and phrases? Language flexibility enhances our ability to think and communicate. You may understand a concept and even know it by another name. But if the current term to describe it is not in your vocabulary, you will be lost when someone uses it in a fast-moving conversation or lecture.

When confronting change, many people react in extremes. They either dig in their heels or lie down and roll over. The ability to be flexible will help you avoid those extremes, both of which are counterproductive. It will also help you keep your balance and make a knowledgeable assessment of the value of the change. You need a clear head to evaluate whether a change will have a positive or negative effect on your business or life.

STYLES OF CHANGE

Overcoming resistance to change is easier if we understand the different ways in which people change. There are five basic ways, and I think of them as styles of change: *incremental, systemic, exception, coercion,* and *pendulum swing.*[1] See if you can recognize your style. Once you are aware of it, you can assess whether it is working for, or against, you.

Incremental

This is the most common style by far, and the easiest to follow. Incremental change means taking the little steps that finally add up to something big. The process is slow enough that we hardly notice.

Exercise is a good illustration. Most of us resist exercising, even though we know that we will feel better if we stay with it. The same kind of inertia keeps us from tackling new technology. It just takes too much mental and physical effort to change the way we do things.

You can overcome your resistance to exercise through sheer determination or desperation. Or you can try the alternative: change the body in stages. You can sneak up on it with slow, methodical steps that eventually lower your resistance. Try this scenario:

Day 1	Think about exercising.
Day 5	Look at pictures of people exercising.
Day 10	Watch other people exercising.
Day 15	Buy running shoes.
Day 20	Put them on and sit on the porch.
Day 25	Stroll out to the corner and back.
Day 30	Walk to the park or drive to a track.
Day 35	Watch other people run around the track.
Day 40	Walk around the track.
Day 45	Run one lap.
Day 50	Buy a running outfit.
Day 55	Run a few laps.
Day 60	Run until you are tired.
Day 65	Running becomes an intermittent habit.
Day 70	You feel good. You tell other people.

If you buy the running outfit and a treadmill the first day you decide to exercise, chances are that both will soon join your other artifacts of failed attempts at change. Corporations make the same mistake; they regularly pay big money for training packages that go largely unused or seminars that soon play to dwindling attendance. I think of it as management by "best-seller."

Keep in mind that incremental change takes a long time to become a regular part of your life. It is like building a wall one brick at a time, with rests in between. Think how tentative you were when first using a cellular telephone or a fax machine. Coming to terms with those devices was simple compared to facing major social, organizational, or career changes. Years of effort are involved. Team building and worker empowerment, for example, can take five to seven years to fully develop and implement. Constant reinforcement helps. Oryx Energy CEO Robert L. Keiser used to zap his executives with a popgun whenever they slipped back into old patterns.

The essence of incremental change is reducing any process to its least threatening increments. Developing computer skills is another example; the smaller the steps the lower the anxiety. The following steps may seem ridiculous if you are computer literate, but look at them as a useful model for bringing about any incremental change. Note how the steps progress and consider how this approach might work with another change you are facing:

Day 1	Watch a friend's child use a computer for a class assignment.
Day 2	Stop by a computer store and sit in front of some computers.
Day 3	Get someone you trust to discuss what kind of computer would fit your needs, or buy a popular book on basic computer use. Sample some computer courses on video.
Day 8	Decide to buy a computer.
Day 10	Start pricing the computer you like. Feel the keyboard and check the design, the amount of memory, the speed, and the clarity of the screen.
Day 20	Inquire about support services (is there a twenty-four-hour 800 number?) for the computer. Check out classes offered by computer stores.
Day 21	List all the tasks that you wish a computer could do. Start reading computer magazines such as *PC*.
Day 22	Start researching software to decide

what is most appropriate for your tasks (writing, keeping files, accounting, investing, art, etc.).

Day 32   Get recommendations from friends, your employer, or the sales staff for a private tutor or check your local community college for computer classes.

Day 35   Get a list from a salesperson of everything you will need for a complete computer station (computer, video screen, software, printer, keyboard, disks for storage, surge protector, connecting cords, paper, mouse, mouse pad, computer cover, keyboard cover, modem, fax, disk storage box, wrist protector, screen saver).

Day 38   Add up all the costs. Read the ads in computer magazines to see if you can buy the package elsewhere at a better price. But remember, you will need more service support than an experienced user.

Day 42   Tell your tutor that you are ready and ask him or her to review your computer package and evaluate it for you.

Day 44   Buy the computer.

Day 45   Turn it on when you are alone and see if you can make sense of the instructions.

Day 46   Set up an appointment with your tutor and start on a few simple procedures (writing a letter, filling out a spreadsheet, loading a program) that you can practice.

Day 47   Nod smugly when a friend mentions that *he'll* never need a computer.

Day 48   Log on to the Internet and greet the world.

Over the years, I have noticed a pattern to the way we change. There are seven basic steps of incremental change. I call the first step *seeing the window*. It's what you experience when you are in the shower or out walking, your mind drifting—and something clicks in your brain. A mental window opens and suddenly you are aware that some change that will affect your future is in the wind—or that you yourself must change. Often that moment of awareness can only be identified in retrospect. If you can learn to catch these glimpses of the future at the first hit, you will have developed a valuable skill.

Whenever you feel tension, ambivalence, conflict, fear, anxiety, or excitement, it is a signal that a window in your mind is trying to open. Give it your attention. What is causing these emotions? Is something changing? Or what changes must you make to relieve them? The most intense feelings about change often occur when you are alone in an isolated environment, traveling in other countries or experiencing a deep loss or trauma.

Some people make the mistake of closing windows and resisting change. How many times have you heard people say:

"I'm too busy, leave me alone!"
"I don't really need to know this."
"This is against my beliefs."
"My boss wouldn't like it."

The machinists at one aerospace plant I worked with preferred to strike rather than be trained to use new computerized tools. Their tools seemed to them the very symbols of who they were. When the company was forced to downsize, they found themselves out of a job, holding old tools in a new world.

When you are helping others to make an incremental change—to accept a new assignment or develop a new commitment, for example—it may require endless conversations and clarifications. There is a need to talk about it to make the event real. If the change is perceived as a loss, talking is one way to take the pain and fear out of it. Discussion lowers anxiety and increases security because the employee perceives that he has value as an individual. A second group of machinists I worked with at Boeing Aircraft was offered unlimited training on the new computerized tools they were required to use and backup work positions if they failed. The environment of security created by their trainer and supervisor resulted in the new equipment's being adopted in record time.

The next step in incremental change is *exploration*. You have seen something through that open window and you are caught by an idea. You begin to gather information. You tell friends and colleagues about the change you are exploring. Some look concerned, some are encouraging. Some debate the merits with you. You begin to build a support network; that is what empowered teams and twelve-step groups are all about. You find people who have made similar changes and quiz them about their experiences. You begin to read books or newspaper and magazine articles on the subject. Maybe you seek out a teacher or counselor, or attend a company seminar.

Your perceptions begin to change. You see familiar things differently. You notice things about people that you overlooked before. This is similar to the change of perception that you experience when you buy a new car; suddenly, you are aware of all the other cars just like it. This step sometimes seems to take forever, but we all need time to build our confidence before making an important change. When you are helping others to change, the exploration step requires you to keep introducing the new idea in many forms until one form "takes."

Eventually you get to the next step, *integration*, the process of embracing the change and making it a part of your belief system and patterns of behavior. Trust your gut instincts, your intuition—even your dreams or nightmares—to help you move through this step. The process requires reflection and clarification because of the emotions that change can evoke: anxiety, ambivalence, a sense of loss, a feeling of being threatened. We often need to talk it out, reassure ourselves, and seek reassurance from others to convince ourselves that we are doing the right thing.

When change triggers such feelings, we can at least take comfort in knowing that we are normal. Change, after all, is a messy process. During mergers or downsizing, the basic trust between employer and employee is usually broken. During periods of change, there are stages of disintegration in a company and stages of rebuilding. But even when we move slowly and painfully, we are getting somewhere.

During the integration process, at first you may want to just experiment, to try the change on for size. If the change is a personal one, you can set up your own process. When I decided to switch careers, for example, I first tested my wings by taking small jobs outside the university—lectures, television commentaries, radio shows, and newspaper articles. Some were paid, some were not.

The hardest step for most is taking the *plunge*, the next step in the process of incremental change. The trip is short but scary. You may momentarily regret what you've done and try to get back to where you were. It's often called "buyer's remorse." Remember the homesickness of camp or the first weeks at college? In retrospect, the job you've just left looks better and better. This is when you need time to adjust, to catch your breath. If people you manage are going through this process, help them to realize that they will have time to regain their balance.

The next step is *landing*. You feel as if you are on solid ground for the first time in days or years. You are exhilarated, confident, and pleased you took the risk and made the change. You feel a sense of independence; you control your own destiny. You look forward, not back, ready to take the next step, the *evaluation* phase. What worked and what didn't work about the change? Is this where you want to be? What next? Evaluation helps to define what is over and what isn't, what makes you feel good about the change and what still makes you uncomfortable. Again, if you are guiding others, ask for their evaluation of the change and how they feel about it. Help them see it has positive value.

Depending on the level of fear or anxiety associated with the change, you may find yourself slipping into neutral about now. You may feel worn down. Change takes a lot out of everyone. A manager may look at a sales division that has just completed a restructuring and wonder where all the enthusiasm went. It's just that body and mind need time to catch up.

When you regain your balance and your energy, you move into the last step of the change process, *sharing*. You integrate all the information and emotions associated with the change, and let go. You feel such a sense of freedom and confidence that you start remarking on it to others. They should make this change too, you think. Use a team that has made a successful transformation to help other units in your business, because their enthusiasm will act as a bridge. Through sharing, the change will become universally accepted. When that happens, it's time to open another window and start the process all over again.

You have probably gone through many incremental changes. Think about an important change in your life during the past five years. Can you re-create the steps of the change? See if these questions help prod your memory:

- When did you first get the idea that a change was in the wind? What was your immediate reaction?
- What process did you go through to complete the change?
- How long did it take?
- What moved the process along and what slowed it down?
- At what point did your feelings about the change turn from negative to positive?
- What caused your feelings to change?

Recalling a past change experience that was successful can reduce the anxiety you feel when preparing for
another change. Talk about that experience with your
family, friends, and colleagues at work. Support groups
of almost any kind can play a role here because they
allow participants to share change experiences. Talking
helps you understand how you and others handle the
different steps of change and will significantly speed up
your next journey, whether you change as a team or as
an individual. It may even be possible to make in a day
changes that once would have taken months or even years.

My journey out of a twenty-year university career
went through all the stages I have outlined and took two
years. I first began to think about leaving the university
during a faculty meeting. Everyone looked either fast
asleep or uninterested, and I had the momentary vision
that they were embalmed (*seeing the window*). A voice whispered to me that if I stayed too long, the ivy would wrap
around me and take over my brain. Until that moment I
had assumed that I would be at the university forever. I
had worked hard to become a tenured professor. I hadn't
thought of being anything else in more than two decades.

Then came the nightmare. At night I began to dream
that I was living in a seedy room near the Seattle waterfront. I was alone because I had dared to give up my
tenured position. None of my colleagues respected me anymore. When I awoke, shaken, I decided to keep teaching
rather than risk abandonment.

A few months later, the idea of leaving returned and
I found myself experimenting with outside lectures. I
tried to find out if there were any happy or successful ex-
professors (*exploration*). The seedy hotel nightmare re-
peated itself several times, always with an image of me
with no one to turn to. Each time I awoke, I resolved not
to resign—but I kept expanding my outside activities until
I was teaching only half-time. The other half I hosted a
radio program on community mental health.

I decided to take control of the nightmare. The next
time it occurred, I willed myself out the door and into a

litter-filled hallway. I encountered the manager and asked him if I could move to the corner room, because it had a view of Puget Sound. I offered, in exchange, to sweep up the hallway. I collected the beer bottles and cans in the stairwells and turned them in for money.

Gradually, night by night, I adjusted the nightmare and dealt with the fears that it generated (*integration*). One night I dreamed I was sitting in my room looking out the window and feeling pleasure at seeing the sunset over the water. I said to myself, "I could stay here forever." The next morning I wrote my letter of resignation to the university. When I packed up my books and research notes (*the plunge*), I felt empty. I took a full-time job at a radio/ television station and realized, very quickly, that I had no regrets (*landed*). The new job exceeded my expectations (*evaluation*). A friend took a photograph of me that month, in a new suit, standing on a dock near my home with my arms outstretched. My nightmare had turned into a dream. When I saw the photo later, I realized that I was somehow welcoming the future.

Systemic

The incremental style of change is the way most of us have handled changes in the past. But systemic change is the change style of the future. It is especially appropriate when a fast and comprehensive response is important. It is deep-seated, enlightening, and often rapid; it lets new thoughts or understandings flood the entire body and mind. Maybe the best examples are visceral: when you know you are in danger; when you know you are in love. Or the instant "Aha" or "Eureka!" when you suddenly hit upon the solution to a problem at work. There is an extraordinarily complete sense of knowing. You can feel it.

Instead of changing one step at a time, you experience a total transformation. You don't, for example, just change your diet or quit smoking; you change all aspects of your unhealthy lifestyle into healthy ones. Examples of systemic change are becoming common. Seemingly overnight, a young adult abandons his pattern of rebellion, evaluates his goals, and suddenly sees his interests differently. The next morning he takes out the earring, buys a suit, and enrolls in school. The entrepreneur suddenly sees with great clarity the shape of the product or business he or she has been struggling to create.

Systemic shifts are very powerful. Norman Cousins wrote about his in *Anatomy of an Illness*, a book that changed the way many people viewed the healing process. Tom Peters and Robert H. Waterman identified the business world's systemic shift to customer orientation when they published *In Search of Excellence*. Writer Joel Barker has described the process as reversing the commonsense relationship between seeing and believing. Instead of "I'll believe it when I see it!" the reverse becomes the rallying cry: "I'll see it when I believe it." As it happens, this is a key element in thinking in the future tense: the ability to see the need for a new product, service, or organizational change without immediately knowing how that need can be met.

When an existing system has been successful (for example, AMA-dominated health care or the all-male military), we are reluctant to make changes. Yet, systemic changes are more common than one might think; we simply fail to recognize them as such. Some examples are lifetime training of workers, downsizing, the diversity push, women in politics, and no-smoking policies. System changes often require a 180-degree turn, a complete reversal of the assumed direction. Look at the actual or potential impact of cable-access channels on the television establishment, or managed care on traditional medical practitioners, or term limitations on career politicians.

It is common for people or organizations that are caught up in a systemic change to perceive it as a threat to their basic identity. Leaders who enjoyed great advantages in the old system can lose much or all of their leverage. When that happens, they become preoccupied with the threat and fail to recognize the necessity for change until it is almost too late. Sears retail and catalog stores were unprepared for the competition of specialty stores in the 1970s. While high-end and low-end discounters prospered, the "middle" that had been Sears's market collapsed.

Think about your own experiences with systemic change, perhaps an organizational shake-up or a merger at your business. In fact, with systemic change, you go through the same seven steps of incremental change— only at a much more rapid rate. Try to identify the window that opened to start the process, your reaction to the prospect of change, and how you finally made it. A heightened awareness of all that you experienced will prepare you for the systemic changes yet to come.

DYSFUNCTIONAL CHANGE

Not all styles of change are equal. Both incremental change and systemic shifts produce authentic and lasting results. But there are dysfunctional change processes: change by exception, change by coercion, and the pendulum swing.

People who change by exception, for example, prefer to inch into the future, resisting every step of the way. Instead of changing their basic belief systems, they create exceptions to the rules of those systems. A racist convinces himself that he is not prejudiced by creating an exception: "I don't like blacks except for Colin Powell." Here are some other statements that reflect change by exception: "I don't like computers, but I can use this word processor." "Most women cannot think logically, but Marie isn't bad." "I don't respect politicians, but our mayor is different." "Education is in trouble, but my child's school is fine." Making exceptions is a way to avoid making a change.

Most of us learned change by coercion in childhood,

when those with power greater than ours applied pressure: "If you don't do this, you'll be sorry." Even as adults, some of us keep experiencing it: "Learn to work with Ms. Calhoun or lose your job." The problem with coercion is that it usually inspires a reaction. Even if the change is positive, we resent it when someone else tries to control us. So we sabotage the change, or refuse to cooperate, or bide our time to get even. Think about all the stories you have read about "disgruntled employees." Their dissatisfaction probably stems, at least in part, from some coerced change.

The success of coercion often depends on its target's having low self-esteem or a hunger for status. Such people can be coerced into doing things that others would resist or reject outright. Coercion also works because of the power of a group to punish rebels and snitches. Nevertheless, coercing change in the workplace is the least effective management style.

The pendulum swing is the style of change practiced by the most rigid among us. It involves going from one fixed system to another, from hierarchy to anarchy, from formal to informal, company loyalty to sabotage, liberal to conservative, addiction to abstention, submission to aggression, loving to hating. The pendulum swing is the preferred style of people who hate ambiguity and want complete control. They see the world in black-and-white terms; there is no room for shades of gray. They don't want to grapple with an issue; they prefer pigeonholing people or ideas.

The obvious problem with the pendulum swing is that it turns off the brain. Any information that might conflict with a currently held opinion or belief is rejected. Pendulum people are always out of balance; they may just as quickly swing in the opposite direction, making true awareness and growth or change impossible.

SURPRISE CHANGES

Change by surprise is in a category all its own. It's not a style of change that you adopt. Instead, sudden changes in circumstances compel you to make a change. Earthquakes, accidents, illnesses, and war are usually unpredictable. A less traumatic surprise may be getting fired without warning. How you respond to it is the important thing.

Several years ago I was fired by a radio station despite my program's very high ratings. I was the only female anchor, opinionated and full of ideas. They cleaned out my desk while I was on the air, handed my belongings to me in a box, and escorted me to the door. I sat in my car thinking about short- and long-term solutions. I found it absurd and ultimately funny. I was forced to rethink my career path, my goals, my behavior—and to make radical changes in my life. Rather than do battle with the station, I proposed a compromise strategy. Now the same executive who fired me regularly brings me in to conduct training for the company and has become a friend.

One way to be prepared for unexpected and unwanted change is to imagine the worst thing that could possibly happen and then think about how you would handle it. I sometimes conduct survival exercises with groups. I ask them to come up with five new jobs they could find to support themselves if they were fired tomorrow, and three new places they could live if they had to leave town. I ask them to imagine what items—poncho, thermos, library card—they would need to survive on the streets if they ended up homeless.

In most cases a group's first reaction is anxiety. Many successful people feel they are one step from disaster. But eventually they laugh and realize they have exaggerated their fears, which can block them from making necessary, and positive, changes. Once you've imagined the worst that could happen to you and recognize that it's possible to survive, change by surprise seems less threatening. If the new career symbol is more a pogo stick than a ladder, we all need to be prepared to handle the ride.

FINDING ALTERNATIVES

Your company has been downsized and you're out of a job. What are five ways you can make a living? List both creative alternatives (what you would like to do) as well as practical alternatives (what you are sure you could do).

Creative Alternatives	Practical Alternatives
_____	_____
_____	_____
_____	_____
_____	

Where are three places you could move to if you were somehow forced to leave your home, town, or region?

_____

_____

_____

The more aware you are that you have alternatives, the easier it will be to make changes.

What I now do (write and lecture) ended up third on my own list of alternatives when I was fired from my last radio station. The fifth alternative was to be a server. I had worked my way through high school and college in restaurants and I knew I could do it. I didn't want to do it, but I knew I could survive. That knowledge buys you the freedom to make necessary changes. An accident, an illness, a business failure—all can compel you to make surprise changes. But the bottom line is this: The fear of change is the enemy of change. If you succumb to that fear, you will also fear the future.

MAKING THE TRANSITION

Remember when: real men didn't eat quiche, we all drove American cars, ice cream came in five flavors and none of them were nonfat, phones didn't ring in cars, Russia was a threat, the Berlin Wall stood, sex was a secret, no one had purple hair, national health care was not a concern, "Made in Japan" meant cheap, and Americans had not walked on the moon?

The world does not stand still, and today the pace of change is more rapid than ever. Be aware of the history of change in your world and be patient with transition. It can take a long time to accommodate change, and the bigger the change, the longer it will take to feel comfortable with it. Try to get past the feeling that change is threatening. We need to see it for what it is, the natural order of things. We do have the ability to separate positive changes from negative ones. Resistance to change is like treading water. It wears you out.

You can improve your response time by staying informed and keeping abreast of all the changes going on around you. Diversify your interests and know what is truly important to you—what you can readily give up and what you want to keep. In times of change, a moral compass is the one thing that will point you in the direction you want to go. Watch out for the barriers to change that lurk in all our minds—nostalgia for an imagined past, lack of awareness, workaholism, arrogance, the need for control or power, perfectionism, lack of confidence, the need to be right, a closed mind, stress, waiting for someone else to change, fear of loss, grief. On your journey into the future, these are the barriers that will trip you up and slow you down.

Understanding the Past to Know the Future

"History's lesson is that it is precisely the times of wrenching change that humankind makes its most significant advances, that the largest enterprises are created, that the richest personal fortunes are built, that the most enduring achievements are recorded."

—MARSHALL LOEB, IN A SPEECH BEFORE THE
CHAMBER OF COMMERCE, SEATTLE, WASHINGTON,
SEPTEMBER 24, 1993

NORMAN ROCKWELL'S PAINTINGS ARE sweet, nostalgic slices of America's past. For a Thanksgiving cover illustration, he painted the family gathered around the dining room table with clean faces, wet combed hair, and lots of smiles. No one is crabby or stoned. Mom is a bit plump, but happy and proud of her cooking. But how real are the images? Sometimes I wonder if Mom might really be thinking, "I had to cook the entire damn meal alone while the men listened to the radio and smoked. I know Junior has been sneaking whiskey; that's why he has that silly smile. On top of that, my girdle is killing me." Dad, proudly carving, might be thinking, "She's overcooked it again, and she's getting fat."

Nostalgia locks us into beliefs about the way things were that may have little or no basis in reality. We remember the warmth of the log cabin and forget the cold of the outhouse. Why is nostalgia a problem? Because it makes us less able to adapt to change. People steeped in nostalgia cannot even remember the present, let alone sense the future. Nostalgia makes us freeze in the head-lights of change.

People who feel overwhelmed or anxiety-ridden by change are likely to retreat into nostalgia. They long to be somewhere else at some earlier time. They imagine a time and a place where "things are the way they should be." Nostalgia is used in advertisements and marketing because it evokes such times and places. I remember a Maxwell House coffee commercial set in small town America around the turn of the century. Men relaxing in an old-time café are sipping coffee out of tin cups while a July Fourth parade passes by. The camera pans to towns-people outside watching the parade, one of whom is an African American, and a warm voice intones, "Every-thing was better back then, even the coffee." For a mo-ment, we believe it. But wait a minute. Think of what that coffee tasted like after the beans in those dirty burlap sacks were boiled in a tin coffee pot. Compare that to a Starbucks latte.

In images like those in the commercial, the past gains power over the present because we tend not to re-member the stress and anxiety of earlier times and events. Our memories are usually positive and selective. This phenomenon is perhaps a survival device, but it can keep us locked into an imaginary world where reality seldom intrudes. This doesn't just happen to individuals; it afflicts entire societies. So much is forgotten or reinter-preted in America that our filmmakers are able to make heroes out of outlaws and redesign Pocahontas to look like a Barbie doll.

If we recognize that nostalgia and anxiety walk hand in hand, then we are able to understand how human be-havior can go awry in times of rapid change. The gloom, the cynicism, the paranoia, and the threats of Armaged-don that emerge in such times—listen, for example, to talk radio—are entirely predictable. Underlying it all is depression or anger, the most common responses to anx-iety. Nostalgia becomes sad rage. We carry memories of "the good old days" in our brains like tree rings, and the "spirits" of the past give them power. It is a mythical belief that what was once right is right for all time.

People caught in the nostalgia trap no longer feel as if they fit in their time and place. Some of them retreat into the woods and arm themselves against intruders. Others join the Ku Klux Klan, the neo-Nazis, or rigid fundamentalist groups and militias, trying to create an environment where they are again in power and everything is under control.

Nostalgia is also a trait of the organizations that I call lodges—everything from corporate cultures to religious sects. Their bonding power often exceeds loyalty to family or country because they create intimacy through shared ideals and beliefs, ceremonies, stories, and legends, and depend on it for their survival. The message is clear: Don't question what we're doing. Just appreciate how long we've been doing it.

Businesses that mistakenly assume the future will be no different from the past usually think that way because of nostalgia. The outcome can be deadly. A few years ago, I worked with a group of independent hardware store owners who were facing increased competition from big chains such as Eagle but seemed blissfully confident. They still ran their businesses in the decades-old tradition of the "local" hardware store, with all that the term implies. They figured their customers would always shop there first and would patronize the big chains only if an item wasn't in stock. But over time, the supposedly happy customers had begun to drift away.

It didn't take long to find out why. In surveys, the customers told the independent store owners not only that the big chains had lower prices, but that the service was better. Women especially felt they couldn't get their questions answered in the local hardware stores—or that the advice they did get was unclear. Men who were not handy with tools felt uncomfortable with the "we all know how to do this stuff" atmosphere of the local stores. The customer base had changed in the direction of busy women and men who wanted information along with their purchases.

Nostalgia is deeply entwined with our own mortality. We cannot imagine the world continuing without us and we deeply want to believe it won't be such a great place anyway. It is somehow reassuring to many people to think that they had the best and it is over. Retirees sometimes brag that their timing was just right, full Social Security and an inflated real estate market. Nostalgia can even become a rationale for welcoming death. If you're dying, it's nice to believe you wouldn't want to stay.

Reading history is a good way to cure nostalgia. You'll be reminded that the good old days weren't necessarily all that good. Lance Morrow, in a *Time* essay titled "The Bad Old Days," made this point. He quoted from an 1854 report in the New York *Atlas*: "Horrible murders, stabbings, and shootings, are now looked for, in the morning papers, with as much regularity as we look for our breakfast . . . Scarcely a day passes that we do not hear of the most outrageous assault with a deadly weapon."[1]

Feeling nostalgic for great leaders of the past? Read up on Millard Fillmore, Franklin Pierce, and James Buchanan, a corrupt and dispiriting procession of mediocre presidents who were spineless when it came to slavery. Convinced that most people were better off in the old days? At the time of the Civil War, the poorest half of Americans owned just 1 percent of all assets; now they own 6 percent. That is very low by European standards, but at least those below the poverty line now live considerably above the bare subsistence levels of other eras. Accurate knowledge of the past produces accurate knowledge of the present and a way to predict the future.

A TIME OF ILLUSION

For many of those who grew up in the 1950s, that decade is wrapped in the golden glow of nostalgia. Families lived carefree and happy lives; we know that from TV programs such as *Leave It to Beaver, Father Knows Best,* and *The Donna Reed Show.* The president was a genuine hero—former general Dwight D. Eisenhower—and everyone trusted him. All those who wanted a job had one, and it was guaranteed for life. Married couples weren't unfaithful; children weren't beaten or molested; there was no rape; African Americans were content with their place. My, how times have changed. Or have they?

In her book *The Way We Never Were,* Stephanie Coontz explodes 1950s myths. Coontz quotes author Benita Eisler: "As college classmates became close friends, I heard sagas of life at home that were Gothic horror stories. Behind the hedges and driveways of upper-middle-class suburbia were tragedies of madness, suicide, and—most prevalent of all—chronic and severe alcoholism. . . ."[2] America was a wonderful country in the 1950s. It just wasn't the placid utopia that a nostalgic nation years later imagines it to have been.

During this "golden decade" African Americans in the South faced legally sanctioned segregation and pervasive brutality. In the North, they were virtually excluded from higher education, unions, and apprenticeships. When Harvey Clark tried to move into Cicero, Illinois, in 1951, a mob of four thousand whites tore his apartment apart while police stood by and joked with them. Native American men aged twenty-five to thirty-four killed themselves at a higher rate than any other population group.

Women workers, so needed in factories during the war years, found themselves purged from the workforce—especially from the higher paying or traditionally male jobs—after the men returned. Sexual harassment and assault were not uncommon. Homosexuals were classified among the mentally ill. Spouse battering was not considered a real crime. Much of what we now label child abuse was normal discipline. Incest was described by experts as a one-in-a-million occurrence, and molestation was considered a rare event always perpetrated by strangers, both of which we now know not to have been true.

Everyone had a duty to marry and reproduce. Bachelors were characterized as immature, narcissistic, and even deviant. Single motherhood was a disgrace, and women died in illegal back alley abortions. There was no mandate for absent fathers to pay child support. Sexual double standards flourished. Prostitutes were available for men, but women were not thought to be decent if they had orgasms. Men were almost never allowed custody of their children because it was thought that they did not know how to care for them. (Even a decade later, as I was lecturing to a group of army officers, a major told me that every woman had a curved bone in her forearm that made it easier for her to hold babies.)

The environment was routinely degraded and polluted. Attitudes toward animal life were unfeeling. Big-game hunters came home with the heads, feet, and skins of lions and rhinos as trophies. Zoos were cement prisons. We decorated our homes with tiger- and bearskin rugs. Women wore leopardskin coats and bought ivory chopsticks for their hair. Individuals with physical limitations or impaired intelligence were shunned. Curbs were not ramped for wheelchairs, and wheelchairs were not allowed in theaters. The mentally ill were warehoused and lobotomized. Eugenic sterilization was common; more than sixty thousand Americans, so-called undesirables, were sterilized in the 1950s. On-the-job accidents were considered the price of doing business or keeping a job.

The 1950s was a time built on illusions. One of the most dangerous was America's view of its place in the world. The Japanese, Koreans, Italians, British, Germans, and French, still recovering from World War II, were barely able to feed themselves. Their cities had been leveled, their factories destroyed, their workforces decimated. Few goods were being manufactured for export.

NOW VERSUS THEN

Try your hand at the quiz that follows. See how you feel about life in the 1990s, compared to the past of your choice. Is it better, worse, or about the same? When you're done, think about whether your beliefs are based on fact or nostalgia.

Subject	Your Vote (better, worse, same)	My Vote (using 1960)
education	_____	same
health	_____	better
life span	_____	better
safety of children	_____	same
treatment of minorities	_____	better
treatment of animals	_____	better
environmental degradation	_____	better
housing	_____	better
world war fears	_____	better
personal safety	_____	worse
social safety nets (SS, Medicare)	_____	better
real poverty	_____	better
individual freedom	_____	better
world starvation	_____	same
world health	_____	better
crime	_____	worse
domestic violence	_____	better
street violence	_____	worse
drug abuse	_____	same
political corruption	_____	better

It took a generation for these countries to begin to compete with America, to export rather than import. During that time we began to believe we were superior, not just profiting from an unusual advantage. We made fun of the cheap paper, tin, and straw goods of Japan, unaware that that was all they had. We seemed to hardly notice when they went from tiny paper umbrellas to first-rate automobiles.

America was, indeed, the richest country in the world in the 1950s, and our economic self-satisfaction during that period evokes a powerful sense of nostalgia. But a return to that decade could be accomplished only by bombing the rest of the world into a preindustrial age and then selling them our products. Similarly, a return to the family life of the 1950s would mean increasing poverty, denying women and children their basic rights, and encouraging racism and classism in all its forms.

If the feeling persists that you, your business, or your family would have been happier or more successful at some other period in history, check it out. Read newspapers or historical accounts from that time and try to discover the way it really was.

LODGE CULTURES

The structure and culture of many of our organizations maintain and sometimes enforce a nostalgic—and unrealistic—view of life and work. Lodges admit only the "right" people, dress them in ceremonial outfits, adorn them with pins and rings, and teach them insider rituals. Within these sealed cultures, the hierarchy is rigid, tradition is revered, and secrecy and loyalty are paramount.

In the past, lodges were usually formed to protect community or class interests. With membership came status and power. As a group, the lodge members could do things that might be more difficult to accomplish alone, such as contributing to or exerting control over a community. Lodge membership could also provide influence or privilege. Some class-based lodges could assure admission to colleges or provide access to jobs and business opportunities from which nonmembers were largely excluded.

Lodges of all kinds pretty much operate the same way today, although some are more extreme than others. In military academies, for example, loyalty to the lodge code that forbids members from "ratting on" one another creates a terrible ethical dilemma when it comes in conflict with the code of honor that demands that truth be told, whatever the consequence. Annapolis, in its last cheating scandal, rewarded cadets who refused to answer questions if their responses might implicate a fellow student. Cadets who told the truth were "separated" from the academy. Those who kept silent to protect themselves or others—in effect, those who lied—were allowed to stay on. "Whistle-blowers" face the same coercive pressures even when they report on company practices dangerous to the community.

Think of a lodge as a cooperative alliance of almost any kind in which the members bond together for power or protection or both. Now, think of these as lodges: the American Medical Association, the American Bar Association, the Army Corps of Engineers, the Forest Service, police and fire departments, military academies, alumni clubs, unions, churches, political organizations, and, especially, the executive group at many American corporations. Each of these shares many if not most of the characteristics that we commonly associate with organizations such as the Elks or the Masons. They are lodges in every way, and when they function like an exclusive club they are major obstacles to change.

Traditional lodges don't do well during periods of rapid change because they are rarely, if ever, visionary. Many of them go out of business. Others survive only by undergoing significant transformations. The Elks voted in 1995 to allow women to be equal members as Lady Elks. Here is a sampler of lodges under the pressure of change today:

Physicians—The medical profession long ago took on the characteristics of a lodge. For generations, many doctors have relied on symbols and myths, dealt with patients in a sometimes arrogant manner, refused outside disciplinary reviews, and decided who could join the club. They have hazed recruits with sleep-depriving hospital internships, gained sometimes unreasonable power over the distribution of drugs and the operation of medical technology, and confined nurses to handmaiden status.

All that is changing. Physicians have so rarely been out in front on major health issues—mental health, smoking, equal rights, domestic violence, child abuse—that respect for their profession has eroded. They are now under pressure from the government that once protected their profession—and from patients, other 'health-care professionals, health insurance executives, and managed-care administrators who no longer accept without question every judgment that a physician makes. Increasingly, patients want a role in defining health or illness and deciding treatment options. Physician groups I work with tell me the result of all these assaults on their power is a deep grief within the profession.

Politicians and lawyers—These architects and practitioners of the law have lost the trust and respect of much of the American public, a sure sign of the decline of their lodges. Frivolous suits or filibusters, perversion of justice, and lax enforcement of professional ethics codes expose old lodge rituals and alliances. Highly publicized cases such as the McDonald's hot coffee spill and O. J. Simpson have educated the public about the weaknesses as well as the strengths of the judicial system. A more sophisticated electorate wants an end to the undue influence of lobbyists and legislative stalemates. Open discussion is replacing the back room in legislation; mediation and arbitration are replacing litigation in the fine print of many contracts.

Academics—Business expert Peter Drucker describes university faculties as the most reactionary of the lodges. He writes: "It is the motto of the U.S. universities that when a subject becomes totally obsolete, then a required course should be built around it." Tenure seems, in the 1990s, to support mediocrity—not independent thought. Consider, for example, the amount of learning that has already shifted from schools to employers, who bring in trainers, consultants, and teachers to improve workforce skills. Entrepreneurs are increasingly designing their own education. The availability of the best of universities through continuing education and the Internet may force academics to change.

Religions—Many religions are lodges of a kind. They operate with a hierarchy, provide stability, and confer status and authority. Their power is through myth as much as faith. Their leadership usually is so homogeneous and their culture so bureaucratic that they are unable to evaluate change, let alone respond to it. Some television evangelists seem to be in tears, already dressed for the end.

The Catholic church in America lost 56 percent of its seminarians in one generation and can expect continued conflict with its followers over issues such as birth control, abortion, and sexism within the church. Alienated urban dwellers more than ever want the faith, support, and community of a church, but not if they are forced to violate their individual integrity. Many people turn to religion in the hope that it will resolve the tensions in society only to find that it exacerbates them.

In the end, the rigidity of most lodges is their downfall. When a lodge is first formed, its structure usually reflects the new vision and vitality of the people who came together to create it. But over time, the structure gradually becomes inflexible and the vitality dries up in traditional mind-numbing rituals, symbols, and misplaced nostalgia. When a lodge becomes irrelevant, people either fight for change, refuse to join, or drift away.

CORPORATE CULTURES

Many lodge beliefs and rituals have worked their way into corporate cultures over the years, creating hierarchies that discourage even the most constructive changes if they threaten the old guard. The company's chief executive and its board of directors understand the rules of the old lodge, and many believe in its myths. Warren Bennis, premier business researcher, found that seven of ten people in an organization will not speak up if their view differs from the conventional wisdom. The cardinal rule of almost any lodge is that you do not bring the old gods down if you want to be one of them.

Several years ago I was invited to lead a series of changing sex roles seminars for Philip Morris. Among the many symbols that hit me as I entered the building were all the vending machines with free packs of cigarettes for the workers as they came and went. Another was the smoke I encountered when I entered the boardroom, so thick I literally could not see. Virtually every man and woman present was smoking. When I very gently remarked on this, they smiled and said it was expected. I understood, at last, the depth of commitment that a lodge can command from its adherents. In this group, membership literally was worth dying for.

The hierarchical nature of the lodge system is especially appealing to corporate America. Almost everyone in an organization craves respect, a chance to move up. In a lodge, if you are willing to pay the price, you can gain a position and the status that goes with it. If there aren't enough positions and titles to aspire to, the lodge can usually create them. Corporations began multiplying the number of their vice presidents in the 1980s.

The lodge can also be relied upon to preserve power and privilege for its oldest members. I was reminded of this when I worked with a large Bell company that was attempting to thin its management ranks by flattening the pyramid. Some executive positions were eliminated through attrition and early retirement. But when the company tried to reduce its management structure from twelve levels to seven, it encountered resistance. The reason was obvious. The reorganization scheme was threatening position and status levels that were part of the lodge system, protected by the usual "old boy relationships." In the end, the reorganization failed. The bottom levels were reduced but the top expanded; the pyramid became a spire on a flattened base. The lions kept their positions on the rocks.

Equally disturbing is the way a well-entrenched lodge system gives an organization's leadership little incentive to look beyond the present. I understood this when I was doing a series of goal-planning exercises with a group of senior union executives. I asked each of them to jot down, anonymously, three goals for the future of the union. I had been raised in a union family, so I expected to see some ambitious goals. But as I blithely recorded the answers on a flip chart at the front of the room, they began to laugh at the results. The goal at the top of almost everyone's list was "To keep the union going until I can draw retirement."

The union officers had little investment in its future because they were focused on reaping the benefits of their own past. In fact, they doubted that the union would survive much beyond their retirement. They didn't think the future was worth their efforts. I left thinking how hopeless it was for this union to undergo any change that might enhance its survival. These union officers had an average of seven to ten years before they would retire. New ideas and new members were not at the top of their lists; their old union model clearly did not have a future.

Corporate leaders who follow the dictates of the lodge are not much better at seeing what must be done. W. Edward Demming, the quality guru, has observed that quality depends on managers who are willing to see what is actually happening in a production process and who have the courage to change it. But when corporate cultures behave like lodges (Demming called them "inner systems"), they frustrate that process. The lodge blocks a manager's ability to see what is happening. Nike's early all-male management, for instance, did not recognize the importance of the women's sport shoe market until 1990. Other manufacturers made the millions that could have gone to Nike.

Use the following list to evaluate your own organization. It can sharpen your ability to see reality despite the lodge's tendency to dissuade you from doing so:[3]

1. What do the leaders pay attention to and talk about? Identify their actual priorities versus what gets lip service.
2. How are rewards and status determined? Who gets bonuses, special trips or opportunities, the best work space, and why? Does performance make the difference, or is it whom you know that matters?
3. Compare what the company's training programs teach its managers with the actual behavior of executives who are the role models. Is their style workaholic, aggressive and secretive, or balanced and equalitarian?
4. How do the leaders conduct themselves—like colleagues or like kings?
5. How does management respond to organizational crises? Who is blamed, who is downsized (management or labor), is there cooperation or conflict?
6. Have the recruitment, selection, promotion, and retirement policies favored one group, or have they promoted diversity? Who has been hired, promoted, sidelined, or fired in the last five years?
7. What is the nature of the organization's structure, systems, and procedures? How long is the rules list, how dense are the regulations? Can you talk to just about anyone? Is there support

---

EVALUATING CHANGES IN ORGANIZATIONAL CULTURES

Here is a list of the extremes of current organizational models. Today, most corporations and institutions are in transition somewhere between traditional and more fluid management styles. Mark the spot on the transition line where your company seems to fit.

Traditional	Transition	Fluid
hierarchical	_____	flat
authoritarian	_____	collegial
status based on		status based on
position	_____	performance
salary levels fixed	_____	salary levels dynamic
closed channels of		open channels of
information	_____	information
adversarial union		
relationships	_____	mutual cooperation
individual oriented	_____	team oriented
silo management	_____	integrated
		management
supervision	_____	support
decisions flow down	_____	in both directions
evaluations flow down	_____	in both directions
limited employee input	_____	maximum employee
		input

---

for empowered team building and risk taking? Does the organizational chart look like a pyramid, or has it been flattened?

8. How do the formal statements of organizational philosophy compare to reality? Does the action match the motto on the company coffee cups? When was it last updated?

9. What impression is created by the company's building and the layout of physical space? Do visitors see a fortress with cubicles for the work-

ers and carpeting that leads to the executives?
Or is it open and inviting?

10. What goes on at company meetings and conferences? Where are they held and who is invited?
What do such gatherings say about who is important, who is worth spending money on?

11. What are the stories that company leaders tell
about important events and people in the organization's history? Who is remembered at special events? What does this tell you about the
company?

LEADERSHIP IN A NEW AGE

Enlightened leadership can change a lodge culture by
changing the assumptions on which the culture is built.
The leader who sets out to do this must have knowledge
of the existing culture and be aware of the organization's
key concerns. The goal will be to re-create a positive
shared vision and trust.

Here are some ways to begin this challenging task:
Get to know your corporate culture. Ask the questions
listed on pages 141 to 143, review the chart on page 142,
become an outside observer, watch the give-and-take in
meetings. Pay attention to both overt and covert behavior. Then answer the following questions:

1. What are the basic underlying assumptions of
how people survive in your company? For example, are employees expected to make decisions or
wait for orders? Do managers tell the truth? Is
straight talk the norm?

2. Who or what drives the group or company? For
example, is customer satisfaction the top priority
or is there something or someone more important?

3. Who is accountable to whom? What are the basic standards and ethics, and are they followed? How important is character?

4. Does the personal and professional behavior of the leaders match the articulated values of the group? How does the executive culture differ from the core culture, if it does?

Review internal surveys from the past and/or conduct new ones to understand the key concerns of your people. Spend your time and money on the first- or second-level employees as well as managers. The lower on the totem pole you reach for answers, the greater the chance that you'll hear important basic information.

Set up focus groups with outside facilitators to identify the issues. When lodge members are asked to list the beliefs and behaviors of their group, they usually cannot because these values are buried in their subconscious. Outsiders and minorities can quickly identify the tenets of a lodge they have observed but not joined.

Get answers from your employees to questions such as "Why am I working here?" and "What are my alternatives?" Learn the top three motivators for your employees and the top three barriers they perceive to personal success in the company. Find out what makes their work difficult.

Find out if their perception of the "real" goal or vision of the company differs from the "ideal" one printed on the brochures. Ask everyone to write down, in their own words, what the business of the organization is.

Many high-level executives assume levels of satisfaction, participation, and trust that do not exist. A few years ago, I was using an electronic system to get instant feedback during a seminar for a regional telephone company. The managers in the audience had buttons at their seats to push in response to questions. Their responses would then appear on a large screen. At one point, the CEO declared that his surveys indicated high levels of satisfaction with the direction in which he was taking the utility, and he urged me to ask questions about trust and satisfaction. When I did, the audience, able now to respond anonymously, recorded very high levels of dissatisfaction among all but the top managers.

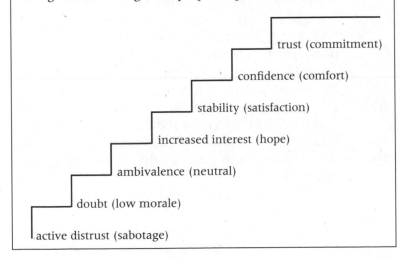

LEVELS OF SATISFACTION

Look at the following "stairs" of feelings and try to judge where your workforce is right now. Test your impression by asking everyone to rate the level of trust in the organization. Trust awareness is especially crucial after mergers and "rightsizings" have damaged employee expectations.

trust (commitment)

confidence (comfort)

stability (satisfaction)

increased interest (hope)

ambivalence (neutral)

doubt (low morale)

active distrust (sabotage)

Every organization has its own specific issues, but wherever I go, employees tell me the same things: They want to learn how to do things, they want to grow, they want to be independent and have control over their work, they want to be connected to others, they want to be involved, they want to have a specific goal or vision of what can be, and they want a driving force or principle to follow.

Weigh each element that emerges in your search for

knowledge and awareness (from the management hierarchy to the allocation of space) and decide which match the future goals of your business and which do not. Watch out for polarity thinking; the most useful answers are usually somewhere in the middle. Try answering the following questions whether you are currently an executive or are just interested in the leadership process:

1. What is your business? Honda decided it made engines, not motorcycles, so it added lawn mowers to its product line. 3M describes its business as "solving problems."
2. What is your top priority? Profit, longevity, competitiveness, growth, quality, new product development, customer service, or something else? SAS decided on longevity, quality, and an empowered workforce. Sony lists the "elevation of Japanese culture and national status."
3. Whom do you have to please—customers, owners, shareholders, regulators, media, or others— and when? Bell Atlantic reduced service time for new connections from fifteen days to a few hours. Nordstrom puts service to the customer above all.
4. What is your relationship to the community? To the environment? Weyerhauser modified its clear-cutting to meet community concerns before new forestry regulations were mandated. Merck believes deeply in social responsibility.
5. What is your relationship to your employees? Many Japanese companies see employees as permanent family members. Some American companies see employees as intelligent but replaceable machines. What will work for your business?
6. Whom are you going to reward and how? On what will that reward be based: seniority, merit, innovation, bottom-line results, or other consid-

erations? Citicorp rewards, with bonuses, employees who are "aggressive and self-confident."
7. What is the long-term goal or vision of this organization? What are the opportunities, obligations, and responsibilities that are involved in reaching that goal? Walt Disney's vision is one of "continuous progress via creativity, dreams, and imagination."

The most heartfelt complaint I hear from workers is that their leaders do not follow through. That may be because the vision they hold is not clear. Using the examples of corporate culture on pages 141 through 143, consider how each of these cultural elements will impact the priorities you just listed.

It always helps to have a metaphor, so let me share what my friend Baron Stewart at IBM calls the "business dance." It seems especially appropriate for managers about to challenge the lodge culture. Think of your employees as dancers, and then ask yourself who is out of step and who needs a teacher? How smooth is the dance floor? You can take the metaphor as far as you want. Who are your partners? Who is leading? Who gets to dance the most? Who creates the new steps? Who are the wallflowers just watching it all move by? Cha-cha-cha.

FIVE STAGES TO RECOVERY

The magnitude of change that we are now experiencing in our society, our economy, and our corporate culture, even if we are not nostalgic, inevitably produces voids. We lose faith in our leaders, our organizations, and ourselves. When we experience a loss, it almost always triggers a period of transition. But we find it difficult to look beyond the void and see the change process taking shape. This common form of pessimism seems to afflict us as a nation. America appears in grief over lost traditions, lost illusions, and lost expectations. Think of what we have experienced in just the last half of the twentieth century: assassinations, riots, Vietnam, Watergate, civil rights upheavals, loss of world status, lost industries, AIDS, changes in sex roles, soaring national debt, and the savings and loan rip-off.

The grief/nostalgia syndrome is also evident among many of our workers and business leaders, who are reeling from the impact of events such as rightsizing, takeovers, foreign competition, and the outright collapse of companies. Learning how both individuals and organizations make it through the stages of grief can help us to better understand how to come to terms with loss, ride out the period of transition and rebuild for the future.

Denial, the first stage of grief, can be seen in entire industries when they are facing reengineering or market and cultural changes that deeply affect their businesses. Timber, newspapers, and health care are examples. Companies or organizations that are in denial will continue on the same track regardless of overwhelming evidence that they are going in the wrong direction. Look, for example, at the behavior of defense industries, department stores, the National Rifle Association, and the Florida sugarcane industry. Warnings of all kinds go unheeded: budget deficits, consumer lawsuits, articles in professional journals, declining stock prices, battles with media investigative reports, what managers see and hear at work every day. Common sense stops being common practice because it only makes sense if it fits your beliefs.

Jim Renier of Honeywell observes in *The Transformational Leader* that the bottom level of an organization usually comes out of denial first and the top level last. The Pentagon denied for years the firsthand experience of troops whose new guns repeatedly jammed or pilots whose planes malfunctioned. The *Challenger* space shuttle disaster was traced to executives of Morton Thiokol, Inc. who refused to believe that certain seals could fail in cold weather even though they had been so warned by their own engineers.

Anger, the second stage, erupts when the damage or loss is finally perceived. Suddenly, there is a demand for explanations, a need for scapegoats. Managers and executives variously blame unproductive workers, trade imbalances, federal policies, the market, unfair competition, special interests, unions, and the weather. Workers blame their superiors, coworkers, foreign competition, and the government. Politicians get angry at each other and lambaste the opposition, the previous administration, immorality, the media.

Rigid thinkers usually seem angrier than those with more open minds. Liberals often intellectualize the complexity of problems and miss the reality, while Conservatives tend to stick to old formulas that are easily understood and generate simple emotions. Tune in to the talk radio shows and you can sense the conflict in the air. Take note of how many callers feel left out or obsolete. Anger almost always stems from a fear that someone is trying to take away something you have, or that you don't have something that others do have.

Bargaining, the third stage of grief, is the last effort to keep things as they are while seeming to change them. A company or organization under siege by its workforce, for example, tries to make a new deal that is as much like the old deal as possible. Boeing Aircraft's board of directors said it would grant a six-million-dollar bonus to its CEO in 1995 if he raised shareholder value. A few months later, Boeing tried to cut its machinists' health-care benefits and the union walked out on strike. Corporate cultures move only inches at a time. They play defensive strip poker with their workers, taking off a shoe here and a sock there, always demanding something in return. Workers increase production, attend team meetings, work overtime, do more with less, but somehow the changes all seem to be in one direction: higher salaries for executives, which make everyone in a company wonder if they are all playing in the same ball-park.

Sometimes the attempts to fend off change are not subtle at all. Insurance companies offer to run the nation's health-care system. Drug companies offer to provide a few vital inoculations at lower prices. The Tobacco Institute talks about American individuality and freedom. Legislation that would allow "almost" clean air, "almost" clean water, and "almost" safe meat is put before the Senate. The Japanese are good models of bargaining. They are masters at avoiding real change. They win their trade wars by losing many tiny battles very slowly while keeping their fortresses intact.

Acceptance, the fourth stage of grief, is a turning point. Reality finally hits, the mind opens, and the entire system seems to shift overnight. People are inspired and energized by the sudden realization that what they have lost is gone forever and it's time to get on with their lives. Workers are eager to do something, anything, now that their companies seem open rather than resistant to change. Everyone has been treading water for so long that even the slightest forward movement is exhilarating.

This can be a time of humiliation or embarrassment for those who have been the most resistant to change. It is not unusual to see top executives depart and new, action-oriented executives take over. But the contrast between business-as-usual and action of any kind can make it seem as if the new management lacks direction. It's like swimming in a sweatshirt race. Tremendous exertion produces very little forward momentum until you take off the sweatshirt. Then you are so light, you seem to zip through the water—until you crash into the end of the pool. Even after the acceptance of change, it still takes time to establish a new direction and a new pace.

Rebuilding is the last stage of grief. Exhilaration is subsiding, things are heading in the right direction, and it is time to plan for the long haul. The major task for managers at this stage is to rebuild trust in the corporate culture that is emerging from a period of transition and change. US West is a model of how to move quickly through the rebuilding stage and achieve good results. When the company underwent realignment in the 1980s, many workers were required to change locations or be retrained for new jobs in team-based divisions. The first reaction was fear and panic. But the company's managers, led by a visionary chief executive, Jack MacAllister, laid out a detailed change plan that gave workers flexibility in choosing their jobs and their work locations. The concerns of spouses and families were considered, and worker input was constantly sought. Regular communications from the company explained the thinking behind the changes. The results, some ten years later, are obvious in this successful Bell spin-off.

Imperial Chemical Industries went through a similar process after purchasing Stouffer Chemical Company, but with mixed results. The merger required that the research-and-development staffs in the two companies be combined. Positions were eliminated, benefits were reduced, and nearly a third of the remaining professionals were moved about. Entomologists, chemists, agronomists, and other researchers suddenly found themselves working in the same division with salespeople and were not pleased. The company's managers made only a minimal effort to inform or solicit input or offer choices, thinking that professionals like these could handle such disruptions. It turned out not to be a good strategy. Rumors flourished, productivity declined, some sabotage occurred, and the research staff suffered a substantial number of defections.

Rebuilding is most successful when there is open and honest communication between employees and management. A popular joke during the merger and buyout frenzy of the mid-1980s made reference to the "mushroom theory of management"—keep everyone in the dark and pour crap over them. Workers who believe they are not being given information on what is really happening lose confidence in themselves and their leaders. In fact, during any period of transition and change, thinking in the future tense requires the ability to think out loud—in other words, to be free to talk about it.

LOOKING AHEAD

As old lodges and organizations fade, what new ones would you like to see take their places? What purpose should a new lodge serve? What kind of group do you want to put in power or keep in power? What lodge are you leaving? What lodge are you joining, or would you like to join? Whom would you let in or keep out? If membership confers prestige and influence, how would you use it? Would you share it? Now imagine it is in your power to take on the lodge mentality of your company. What would you change? What would you keep? Why? What new alliances could you form that would benefit both your company and your community?

The company, business, or individual that stands still, shrouded in nostalgia and the lodge mentality, is denying the inevitability of change, the future. Only when we let go of the past and its illusions can we plant our feet more solidly on the ground of the present. We have to let go of much of our yearning for another time or place to create room for this time and place and for the future.

Doing More with More or Less

"Humans are wonderfully different and marvelously alike. Human beings are more alike than unalike. Whether in Paris, Texas, or Paris, France, we all want to have good jobs where we are needed and respected and paid just a little more than we deserve. We want healthy children, safe streets, to be loved and have the unmitigated gall to accept love. If we are religious, we want a place to perpetuate God. If not, we want a good lecture every once in a while. And everyone wants someplace to party on Saturday nights."

—MAYA ANGELOU, IN A SPEECH AT OHIO DOMINICAN COLLEGE, DECEMBER 9, 1993

THE CURRENT TREND IN the expenditure of human energy is its increasing effectiveness. We *can* literally do more with less. It is rarely what we do or how much we do that tires us now; it is our mind-set in relationship to what we do. It is our sense of security.

Energy and security, what does one have to do with the other? Both are necessary conditions for coping with our complex new world, the dazzle, the fear that we are reeling out of control. It is hard to be optimistic about the demands of the future when you are tired.

Security is the feeling that you have what it takes to survive and prosper, to pursue work and happiness. Security creates motivation by reducing anxiety and increasing hope. People who feel safe enjoy heightened levels of physical and mental energy, enabling them to respond to the intense demands that change makes on their bodies and minds. People who feel unsafe lack motivation, tolerance, compassion, and the ability to innovate.

What makes us feel safe—or unsafe—today is different from what it was in the past. The incredible growth of television into a national and international nervous system has heightened anxiety. If you watch a lot of television news, you can come to believe that you live in a cruel and dangerous world. You discount your real-life experiences. "News" magnifies and exploits violence, mayhem, and human tragedy, and we lose our perspective.

Ordinary contact with fellow human beings can also erode our energy and threaten our sense of security, especially under the new, more sensitive rules of engagement that we are expected to follow. We have expanded our concept of who deserves respect. When an obese person moves toward us, we can no longer simply write him or her off to gluttony. We now have to think about what Richard Simmons would say, or Oprah, or Susan Powter. We are expected to be understanding.

More and more people claim they are "victims." Street people make demands from the sidewalks and doorways for our attention and charity. We are cautioned not to pass judgment on people who are in trouble unless we know everything about them. Our conscience becomes confused. All this takes far more energy than a quick retort, silence, or avoidance.

Our relationship with time contributes to our unease. Nomads knew hours by the sun and days by the stars. Only the wealthy kept track of time. Now there are clocks everywhere—in cars, on microwaves, in televisions and telephones, even under water. They drive us in ways that sundials and even mill whistles could never drive our forefathers. We rush down airport corridors and panic at delays. We sleep, on average, an hour a night less than people of just a generation ago. Some of us begin our commute before light and don't return home until after dark.

We think of time as money. We move too fast to be fully aware of who we are and where we are going. We no longer seem able to define satisfaction, success, or security. I was reminded of this a few years ago when I was invited to speak to an organization of men who had become millionaires and CEOs before age forty. They were meeting at a luxury hotel in Newport Beach, California, and they asked me to speak on "Self-Esteem in the Jungle."

My first comment was a question: "What jungle are you gentlemen referring to?" They answered: "The corporate jungle!" This was the 1980s, the time of leveraged buyouts and mergers. The fear of takeovers was in the air. "It's a jungle out there," they told me. I asked the executives what they were afraid of, what was dangerous in their jungle? "Is it the elevators? The parking lots? The freeways? The boardrooms?" They answered, "All of it!" Their stress levels were out of sight.

So we talked about how man defines danger, and I suggested that without realizing it, they might actually *want* to feel on the edge, indispensable, almost at war. Why else, I asked, did they use terms of war when discussing takeovers and evoke images of gunslingers in boardroom encounters? After some considerable discussion, I finally got my answers. They were not really in any danger at all, but they loved the feeling of being in battle, hunters and warriors at heart. Whenever it appeared that they were winning, they lost that feeling. So they re-created the illusion of danger. Danger gave them an adrenaline rush. It made them feel important. They had no idea how to live with feelings of safety.

For many of us, however, feelings of insecurity are real. We seek to allay those feelings in material ways: by competing for better jobs and bigger salaries, by acquiring more expensive cars and fancier houses. But after centuries of chasing goods until we no longer can store them or dispose of them in landfills, it is time to start working on new solutions. The old ways of creating safety worked well when jobs were relatively secure and career paths were relatively straight, but no more. Now we have to fight a different kind of battle with different skills to gain security and material rewards.

ENERGY AND SECURITY AT WORK

Workplace pressures of all kinds can contribute to anxious feelings. Past generations worked harder physically. Think of the labors of the farmer or the factory worker decades ago. But we are working harder mentally. Communication, negotiation, diversity, quality control, marketing, managing, and innovation take up far more brain space than planting seed and harvesting crops. We are worn out by anxiety, not physical labor.

When we factor in the fear that America's economic well-being is in decline, that the nation is losing ground in global competition, and that the search for a job is getting tougher as certain skills become obsolete, the picture is complete. Suddenly we realize that lifetime employment has become a memory—and we no longer have a farm to keep us going in hard times.

What this means to your sense of security is clear. If you stay in a declining industry—even in a good job you love—you may not survive until retirement. Worse, your skills may not transfer to the next workplace. The same is true of the persons you manage. A machine tools specialist has no future in microchip manufacturing without additional training. If *The Graduate* were filmed now, the whispered word would be *ceramics*. What do you know about integrated circuits and semiconductors?

More Americans now make computers than all forms of transport, more Americans work in accounting firms than in the whole energy industry, more Americans work in biotechnology than machine tools. The movie industry employs more people than the automobile industry. Twice as many Americans make surgical and medical instruments as make plumbing and heating products. Tourism is the number-one industry in the world.

The jobs of the future will be mental, not manual. I compiled the following list of the most promising "knowledge" job areas of the future from Canadian economist Nuala Beck and other forecasters:

- Information services, software sales and development, computing equipment, photonics
- Commercial research, development and testing labs, scientific and control instruments, optical fibers
- Pharmaceutical, biotechnology and gene research, marketing and sales
- Business, trade and vocational schools, teachers, administrators
- Engineering, architectural and surveying
- Educational research
- Accounting, auditing, financial planning, credit data
- Theaters, film, writers, arts administrators
- Transportation, aircraft technicians, flight engineers, travel agents, truck drivers
- Funeral services and crematories
- Business management and consulting services, employment interviewers
- Radio and television broadcasting, directing, producing
- Radio, television, and communications equipment
- Guided missiles, space and vehicle parts, robotics
- Semiconductor sales and manufacturing
- Advertising, marketing
- Hospitality industry (hotel management, chefs)
- Credit agencies

- Hospitals, medical care and diagnostics, medical technology
- Health services (physicians, dentists, dietitians, chiropractors, nurses, opticians, medical records clerks, physical therapists)
- Surgical and medical instruments and supplies
- Legal services, corrections officers
- General social services, psychologists, social workers
- Child care, elder care
- Public finance, taxation and monetary policy
- Government administration
- Environmental consulting and equipment, waste disposal

Many, if not most, of the jobs in these areas will not require the traditional four-year liberal arts college degree. But they will require technological and production skills, and they will demand a higher level of competence even at the entry level. The burden of preparing workers is expected to fall increasingly on companies themselves, rather than high schools and colleges. IBM's CEO, Lou Gerstner, says that U.S. businesses already spend $30 billion a year on remedial education.

Those with college degrees will more often find themselves in combination jobs or unusual partnerships: lawyer-scientist, engineer–interpersonal relations specialist, engineer-marketer, or programmer-financial planner. Think up some additional combinations, using this list of future industries:

Fiber optics	— Magical use of light beams to carry information through glass fibers smaller than a human hair and capable of transmitting entire encyclopedias in seconds
Photonics	— Using networks of telephones

	to link computers and provide instant data worldwide
Space colonization	— Solar satellites, the new frontier of asteroid mining, hunting, gathering, and living
Alternative energy	— Ethanol, methanol, compressed natural gas, liquid hydrogen, propane
Nanotechnology	— A theoretical process for building everything (homes, food, cars, computers) out of individual atoms
Lasers	— Computer-guided beams for manufacturing, surgery, dentistry
Genetics	— Genetic engineering (food, drugs, body parts and processes) to eliminate congenital defects and inherited diseases

Your future success in the workplace will depend on your having "new economy" skills, even if you are in a secure business or industry that is part of the old economy. If you are on the verge of making a change, look for a company that is part of the new economy. Start by asking what kind of knowledge is necessary to work in this business or industry and where it will take you. Nuala Beck suggests a critical look at the products, the services, the managers, and the appearance of the offices, then see if you hear a little voice saying, "This place is dying, get out of here!"[1] Keep in mind that small entrepreneurial companies are growing faster and offer more opportunity than the big corporations of the past.

You can prepare for this process by spending a day observing the world that you now live in. Count the new services or technologies that were not there when you graduated from high school. Walk through your home or office and count the microchips. Sit in your car or office and look at the new accessories. Walk through the malls or flip through the catalogs and try to predict which stores will be gone next year and what will take their place. Design your own career. For people under thirty, chances are that their jobs don't even exist yet.

CREATING ENERGY AND SECURITY

If security is no longer a given in our lives or our workplaces, clearly we must look to ourselves to provide it. How can we best use our energy to create security? Here are a few suggestions. Some have special application to the workplace or the art of management. Others apply more directly to personal relationships or individual development. But all are useful in learning to deal with insecurity and energy drain.

Observing Energy

You can feel a company that is alive. Some people walk into a room and the motivation level goes up. Others walk into a room and the motivation level drops. Become an observer of such energy shifts. Sit in an office meeting, on a couch at a social gathering, or just at your own kitchen table and watch the energy level rise or fall depending on who enters the room. What do you think is happening? Why? At a meeting, notice how that meeting is run. Does it heighten your energy or drain it? Are there obvious ways the meeting could be run so that its outcome would be more positive?

For example, many teachers entering a traditional classroom took all the energy out of it in the days when the student-teacher relationship was pretty much one-way. They controlled the questions and the information. They controlled the grievance procedures. A good two-way relationship between teacher and students energizes a classroom.

Similarly, many athletic coaches have changed their tactics from control and sometimes humiliation to empowerment, self-esteem, and team-based motivation. Most of the old "exalted" bullies are gone because fear and intimidation are limited motivators. The sources of human energy have changed. You now need to be able to sense people's needs on an emotional level. When the going gets tough, the tough get sensitive.

Analyze the people in your life who motivate you in a positive way. What are the differences between those who reduce your energy and those who increase it? How can you be a source of positive energy to the people you manage? Apply the same test to people who sell products, those providing you with services, or the presenters at training seminars. The give-and-take of positive energy is the key to peak performance.

Technology as a Friend

Think of the energy that was expended when people did errands on horseback at the turn of the century or laundered their clothes on a washboard. Enter technology, the great energy saver. Make it your friend. Determine your technology comfort zone and it will cooperate.

Computerized navigation systems that rely on satellite signals now help you stay on course in your car or boat. Road Scholar makes a system called City Streets for Windows. You plug in the location of your appointments or errands and it helps you establish a route, prints out a map, and provides traffic reports. One navigator accessory even reminds you when to turn, sounds a warning if you stray from the designated route, and then reroutes you. It will be harder to get lost. Men will never again have to ask for directions.

I live in a "smart house" because I am married to a "techie." He is a marine attorney who runs an international seafood and water-quality business. I can tap into our home computer system from Hong Kong and turn off the heat or turn on the sprinklers. I can even let out the dog. He has a microchip on his collar, his own speakerphone extension, and his own door. I can tell from a signal when he is back in the house. But just in case, I have a neighbor who provides backup (new systems are rarely foolproof). My husband can type a memo into his computer with instructions to fax copies overnight to dozens of fishing boats scattered on the world's oceans. Each boat can fax back data in time for the next day's business.

Technology is dramatically changing not only the kind of work we can do but also where we do it. LINK Resources, a New York–based research firm, estimates that 50 million Americans now work full-time in home offices. Many two-worker couples are attracted to this lifestyle as a way to alternate or share their work week and raise a family. Where I live, people who are at home working are part of the community again. Taking a break from our keyboards, we meet and talk at an espresso bar right next to the feed store. We can buy day-old chicks and get "wired" at the same time. In a way, it's a return to the community I grew up in where farmers met to exchange the news of the day.

How would your life change if you could do most of your job at home or from a distance via a computer hookup? Even though these systems aren't perfect now, someday they will be. Don't allow a fear of technology to drain your energy. It is a steep learning curve and the payoff takes time. But once you have mastered it, it becomes an amazing source of positive energy. You will have the secure feeling of being able to keep up with the children.

Putting the Customer to Work

Dialing direct, using ATMs, depositing an overnight letter in a Fed Ex drop box, and taking a home pregnancy test are all examples of the customer's doing the work. Sometimes it takes getting used to. Motorists at first resisted pumping their own gas, but then they began to appreciate the convenience and the time saved. Multitasking conserves a lot of human energy, so it is a driving force in the new economy.

In fact, this strategy can save energy for customer and business alike. As robots and computers do much more, expect to see fewer clerks and attendants but more easy access to information. Also expect to learn the necessary new technology and self-service skills. Ultimately, we should experience fewer of the old frustrations—for example, not getting all the data we need, standing in line, dealing with disinterested clerks or slow attendants. The lost human contact may be a negative or a positive. You get to decide.

On the Cutting Edge

In the new economy, don't expect to be taken care of by your large corporate employer, even if you go along with your company's program. Your job and security will depend on your own competence and work skills, not on the management hierarchy that you might seek to please. That makes you responsible for staying on the cutting edge when it comes to skills development and knowledge of your business or profession and the market in which you compete. Assess your skills, find good teachers, and make time for self-improvement.

Be aware that people who are below you in skill level will always apply upward pressure in times of change. You must do the same. If you try to hold on to work you can easily do that someone on a lower pay scale can also do, you will lose. Physicians, for example, who try to block nurses with advanced training from using medical technology previously reserved for them will lose. Registered nurses who block licensed practical nurses or nurses' aides will lose; nurses' aides will find patients taking over as well. Push yourself and your profession to higher skill levels while letting go of work that others can now do.

Exercise your brain in new ways to keep it fit, just as you do your body. You can count on traditional education or try one of the Neural Gyms that are opening around the country. Mind gyms use electronic systems that stimulate visual and aural parts of the brain, triggering the kind of cerebral adventures that seduced Socrates, Thoreau, and Timothy Leary. One brain exercise client offered this description in *Newsweek*: "There is a moment about five minutes into a brain-gym workout when the rhythm of the flashing lights on your eyes and the soothing sounds of a running river over your headphones becomes indistinguishable from the beating of your heart and the rise of your chest. Deep in your mind physical sensations start to fade and reality rushes away like gas escaping from a balloon, leaving behind a sense of tranquil isolation."[2] Brain salons are perhaps the next stage in our search for sources of positive energy. Smart vitamin and mineral pills are already on the market.

Continuing Education

Teaching the "work ethic" would have once seemed silly, like teaching people to eat or sleep, but it will be essential to stimulate our national energy. Too many American students are not getting the work experience needed to thrive in the new economy. Academics will never be sidelined, but vocational skills and social skills must be given greater attention. Early work training in our schools could be modeled after programs in Germany, Sweden, or Japan. Swedish students begin the work experience in the first grade. All the programs are aimed at providing a smooth transition from school to the workplace. It is extremely damaging for a society when too many of its people don't know how to work.

We already have some models of our own. There are

out-of-school programs all over the country teaching Work Appreciation for Youth (W.A.Y.) in the way we once taught geography or algebra.[3] Students are given their first paid jobs and are taught time management, money management, and pride in work skills. Disadvantaged students, when offered computer classes, absolutely excel.

Community colleges and corporations can fill in the work skills gap for adults while we improve the secondary school system. Vocational education and experience must be expanded in every practical way to help us build high-performance, adaptive workers. There is more to life than work, but without work, life is considerably harder.

There is no greater source of positive energy and security than the knowledge that you can do your job. But in today's rapidly changing world, education has to be an ongoing process. It has truly become an assignment for a lifetime. You may be ninety-five, in a nursing home, with three days to live, and someone will be urging you to learn a new telephone system. "Help!" you cry. "Leave me alone, I'm not going to make a call!" But why not give it a try? Who knows—we might have a straight line to the hereafter by then.

Communication and Negotiation Skills

Half your energy and a lot of your security are lost through an inability to communicate or negotiate easily. This is especially true in moments of conflict or dilemma. Most of us end up trying to avoid conflict because it seems easier that way. But speaking honestly and openly in such situations immediately lifts tension and makes energy flow.

Conflict resolution is important in a society where rapid change has created tension, and we are doing more of it. Unions and management are putting their old adversarial roles behind them, and mediation is becoming common. Even children in kindergarten are being taught how to diffuse anger and be mediators. We are all learning how to control ourselves as well as to manage those who cannot communicate easily. This is important because the way in which people talk together in organizations is central to their ability to work together. Leaders need to notice and increase the time they spend resolving people issues. This is even more critical when centralized management is relaxed and the hierarchy flattens. Then, dialogue becomes the glue that holds the organization together.

A consulting group operating from MIT and Harvard Law School is marketing Socratic Dialogue as a tool for organizational change, problem solving, and internal communications.[4] Socratic Dialogue assigns participants new roles, sets up hypothetical problems, and forces people to decide what they would do and explain why. It can be a welcome alternative to traditional management meetings in which participants too often give canned and predictable responses.

To conserve your energy and sense of security, notice who or what creates conflicts for you and decide what you can do about it. Figure out how much of the problem is yours, not coming from outside. Check whether your myths or perceptions are playing a role. What has changed or refuses to change? Again, maybe the simplest solution is just to talk about it.

Take Action

Treading water drains your energy and deadens your motivation. That is what happens when you find yourself "plateauing," or feeling that your job or career is going nowhere. It's the sense that you are stuck, and it creates a dull ache that lasts until you act to resolve it. It can be a way of resisting change or the end result of not knowing which direction you want to take. Examine your alternatives, explore your opportunities. Where do you want to be five or ten years from now? What can you do now that will point you in that direction?

Entrepreneurs are always thinking about the next deal before the current one closes. Inventors always think beyond their current projects. Authors think about their next book when they are only halfway through the one they're writing. Don't stay comfortable too long. As one door is closing, open the next one. Imagine that your current job or lifestyle will end in six months and conjure up a new one. You may be able to stay where you are forever, but you need to be ready to move. This flexible mind-set is a characteristic of someone who is not afraid of change. It is the perspective of a pioneer.

Open Information

We used to run large parts of our lives, our government, and our businesses in secrecy. Now businesses increasingly open their books and their files to employees and reveal more about themselves to their customers and the public. General Electric rates managers on a one-to-five scale of "boundarylessness," an open flow of ideas. Government agencies, however reluctantly, are making more information public sooner. We are moving into a communication and information age in which the guiding principle will be to tell people what they need to know as soon as possible. This is as true for family members hesitant to be candid with an adopted child as it is for the doctor discussing options with a terminal patient or for a business wrestling with a merger decision.

Keeping secrets is a major energy drain on individuals as well as organizations. Look at the tobacco companies. They could save millions of dollars in litigation costs and man-hours if they just came out and admitted that tobacco is addictive. Why maintain such expensive illusions?

Evaluations and Reviews

These days, people need to know where they stand. The suspicion that we are being deliberately kept in the dark is a threat to our security. Even some employees who once dreaded yearly evaluations now ask for monthly reviews. They want to be able to chart their progress and their job security on a constant basis. They don't want unhappy surprises like sudden termination after months of unwittingly repeating the same mistakes.

An increasing number of American companies are using 360-degree feedback: peer review by coworkers and evaluations that go up the organizational structure as well as down. They provide a sense of real communication and participation by everyone that increases motivation and security. The same process is under way in our personal relationships. We shouldn't have to wait for the divorce papers to arrive to say, "I didn't know you were unhappy." We now try to notice each other's feelings and to communicate openly and honestly.

Financial Sophistication

Money, according to mythologist Joseph Campbell, is "congealed energy." We can unleash that energy only by learning to manage our money. We work, after all, to acquire money and the things it can buy. It is not the only motivator, but it is a strong one. If we are to expend so much time and energy making money, it is only common sense to know how to spend, save, and invest it wisely. It is essential to our security.

Expect more employees to put "classes on investing" at the top of their lists when their companies ask them what kind of training they would like. These people have figured out that in a capitalist system they need to know how money makes money. Money can often protect them from an otherwise uncertain future. The unprecedented movement of bank account savings to mutual funds is an illustration of this thinking.

Schools can do better in this regard. We have just begun to teach personal finance in high schools. It must be a core subject. We need elementary classes in investing. Too many of our children do not grow up in families where compound interest and overhead are dinner table subjects. There are scores of banks and magazines on investing and money management at every level of sophistication. Check them out. Financial advisers abound. Talk to a good one. Company profit-sharing and pension plans are becoming incredibly complicated as employees are offered a wide variety of investment choices. Keep informed of your options and opportunities. Save and invest as a matter of nature for an uncertain world. It's your money—and your future security.

Family Friendly and Flextime

We Americans love to work, and we are, given world-wide comparisons, extraordinarily productive. But we also are stressed and exhausted. In her book *The Overworked American*, Juliet Schor reports that we are averaging 160 more hours a year at work than in the 1960s. But that is only half the problem. The other half is the impact on home and family obligations, especially as more and more women work. Fewer adults are available to meet the usual demands: children's needs, housework, maintenance, elder care, family illness, and so on. The answer to that problem is to allow more employees to work part-time or on flextime. Managers should stay in touch with the needs of their employees when developing work schedules.

Europeans are already increasing part-time positions (30 percent of Dutch workers, 16 percent of German workers), both to respond to lifestyle demands and to absorb the unemployed. American companies, calculating that overtime is cheaper in the long run than hiring more people, traditionally have favored pushing fewer workers harder. But employee stress and the phenomenon of self-managing workers may alter those calculations. Schor reports that the number-one demand in a poll of

American workers was "no more overtime." In all probability, the United States will eventually be forced to adopt a more European model. Studies show that the average work week in Europe is thirty-five hours versus our forty-seven. Perhaps it goes without saying that greater flexibility in work schedules creates positive energy in the workplace and greater feelings of security among workers who do not have to sacrifice their personal lives to keep their jobs.

KEEPING YOUR LIFE IN BALANCE

You get very little sympathy these days for not managing your own time and stress. A generation ago people would say, "Poor George, worked himself to death, good man." Now they say, "What a fool, couldn't keep himself in balance." Your spouse doesn't take responsibility for your diet anymore, and neither does your mother. They smile and say, "It's your choice, dear." This new independence may reduce nagging, but it also obliges you to manage yourself.

Outplacement and career counselor Alene Moris created a pie chart as a way to check your current blend of options, rewards, and obligations and decide what to plug in or unplug. The chart divides your life into various combinations of three basic elements:

1. You as an individual. How do you feel about yourself, your physical state, your spiritual being, and your intellect? How much time do you spend on each in an average week?
2. Your relationships. How is your time divided? What portions are committed to your partner and family, extended family and friends, colleagues and coworkers, and the people or groups you count on for support?

3. Your lifework. How is your time divided among a variety of elements such as your work, community activities, home and personal maintenance, and leisure activities? Do all of these aspects of your life and relationships revolve around your values? Values are the organizing principles that determine the relative importance of your activities and guide your choices about how best to spend your time and energy.

These divisions are rarely equal. Circumstances may require us to put more time and energy into work or

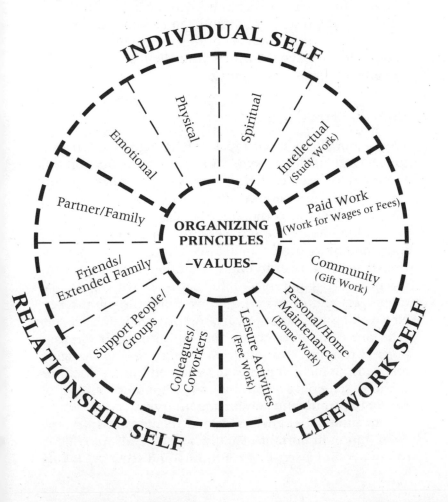

more into family, for example. But all three divisions interact with each other. We no longer separate work and home, we now integrate them. Positive energy generated in one feeds the others; an energy-draining crisis in one can have a negative impact on the others. Ask yourself how well you are keeping these pressures and rewards blended. Draw a blank pie chart and divide it into the same slices as they relate to how you are currently spending your time and energy. What do you feel is in balance? What is out of balance? Are there changes you could make that would be in greater accord with your values? Now make an "ideal" future life pie for comparison. You may not always be afforded the luxury of choice either in the present or as you head into the future. But try to keep your life puzzle put together to prevent stress and anxiety, to avoid wasting your time, and to achieve the greatest degree of security.

Support Networks

We are not alone in our rapidly changing and often confusing world. A lot of people are in the same boat on this bumpy ride, faced with the same difficult choices. Fortunately, there are people who can help us make them. When workers in corporate America lost their guarantees of lifetime jobs, there was a rise in the formation of more and more professional associations. Such organizations have resources to offer job hunters, and their conferences are good places to network with potential employers and others who know about the job market. Networking has become very sophisticated. Job seekers who are computer literate can tap into e-job services, posting résumés, scanning job listings, and exchanging job leads. Some companies have joined the on-line procession, screening applicants by computer instead of reading résumés and conducting interviews.

In times of change, personal relationships become even more important. Family and friends provide a safety net and a sense of continuity and security. Taking good care of these relationships can mean support when we most need it. If you pride yourself on being a loner, you may find that independence wears pretty thin when things fall apart.

Even if you are not job hunting, networks of all sorts can make your life easier. There are service providers such as massage therapists, pharmacists, librarians, tailors, and others who now make home or office calls to people whose hectic schedules leave them time-deprived. Food vendors will deliver lunch or a complete dinner. Computer consultants are on call twenty-four hours a day for at-home telecommuters. New services such as 1-800-ALL-NIGHT handle virtually any crisis. More and more office complexes and health clubs boast of having everything from shoe repairs to mechanics on the premises. On "vendor day" at Nabisco headquarters in New Jersey, you can get a picture framed, make a bank deposit, or sign up for lawn care.

Portfolio Professionals

British management consultant Charles Handy, in his book *The Age of Unreason*, describes a whole new category of workers who are creating their own energy and security. "Portfolio professionals" are so named because they have portable skills they can offer to a variety of employers in a variety of ways. They run projects, solve problems, develop strategies, and handle other specialized assignments.

These men and women have basic professional or technological educations combined with real-world business experience. They have broadened their knowledge by moonlighting, consulting, or joining in entrepreneurial ventures. They are willing to be flexible—to make lateral moves within the same corporations, to change industries, to move to smaller companies, to launch businesses. They are also willing to take a break—a sabbatical, a return to school, some time with nonprofit work. They are good at presenting their ideas to others. They are proficient at networking. They thrive on unpredictability.

Geographic adaptability, at least in the early years, is important. Newly graduated MBAs intent on becoming "portfolio professionals" often look overseas for their starts. They wave foreign flags at their graduation ceremonies to let everyone know where they are heading. Trips that were once rewards for years of studying are now part of serious job searches. One estimate is that 25 percent of American college graduates will seek jobs outside the United States. Their destinations are not the Europe of a generation ago but Mexico, Brazil, Argentina, Tokyo, Hong Kong, Vietnam, and India. The "cowboys" go to the wild east of Eastern Europe and the former Soviet Union.[5]

Professionals with global résumés do not count on climbing ladders—they ride those pogo sticks. They move from project to project or create businesses that appeal to their interests and satisfy their income or lifestyle requirements. They share a kinship with salesmen, consultants, writers, artists, actors, and others who risk living under feast-or-famine conditions. They blur the lines between work and adventure.

There are negatives. Interim executives don't have much clout. Income may fluctuate significantly. The greatest demand will be for specialists who can solve specific problems on tight schedules; generalists can expect to encounter heavy competition. Companies using "portfolio professionals" may decide to operate slightly understaffed and end up with a less loyal workforce as a result. Managers will need superb personnel skills to draw the right kind of talent from an ever-fluctuating pool of workers. But portfolio people are more than just a new kind of temp. They offer organizations a corps of independent professionals who can dive into jobs, work effectively, and then easily swim away. Their presence can reinvigorate corporate cultures and heighten a company's energy level and competence.

Sense of Humor

If you had to choose only two qualities to get you through times of change, the first should be a sense of self-worth and the second a sense of humor. Anatoly Scharansky and Nelson Mandela have both said that humor was a powerful weapon in dealing with the horrible conditions of their years in prison.

Humor helps us deal with absurdities, whether they exist in our personal lives or in our businesses. It allows us to lower our tension, our anger, our pain, and our stress at all the demands we must meet and changes we must make. It renews energy and renews trust in ourselves, others, and our world. There is also a close relationship between humor and creativity: Both require imagination and the ability to suspend judgment. In children there is a measurable correlation between humor and intelligence. Smart people laugh. People who laugh feel good.

Management Styles

The new management mantra is "Get out of the way"; that is, eliminate the bureaucracy and the barriers that discourage the efficient use of human energy. Peter Drucker describes an effective leader as one who knows that "the ultimate task of leadership is to create human energies and human vision." Management styles based on control, coercion, manipulation, and crisis suck energy out of people. Workers forget how to think, communicate, operate without supervision, or innovate.

Companies that operate on the new model rely largely on self-managing groups of workers. These teams hire (whether unionized or not) their own coworkers, set up assignments, make sales calls, solve quality problems, select suppliers, visit customers, work through grievances, and even eat together. There are no job classifications. Workers cross-train and are multiskilled and able to do any job in the plant from management to maintenance. This model has become common in Germany and Sweden.

Think of the new workforce as a self-motivating entrepreneurial chorus of talents committed to making the company music. It will require managers who:

- Treat everyone with respect.
- Are good interviewers.
- Don't get hung up on educational backgrounds (performance counts more).
- Show zero tolerance for racism or sexism.
- Establish shared, known, reality-based goals.
- Focus on quality and service to develop commitment.
- Have a bias toward action and pay people for results, not the time they put in.
- Develop team-based workplaces where appropriate.
- Are computer literate and have a global mind-set.
- Provide employees with opportunities to change jobs; reduce or rotate dull, routine, repetitive work; build an adaptable workforce.
- Nurture ideas from within, encourage innovation, accept mistakes, give praise.
- Help employees develop negotiation and mediation skills.
- Organize extensive training and education activities.
- Develop financial education and investment programs.
- Establish multiple reward tracks that represent company goals.
- Insist on in-depth, thoughtful hiring procedures and probation periods.
- Hire smart people who get along well with others.
- Plan and make known transition processes and avoid crises.
- Open up the information and communication systems.

- Encourage a hands-on approach and collegial relationships.
- Reduce the hierarchy, flatten or rotate management, make performance rather than promotion the goal.
- Conduct frequent employee evaluations so everyone knows how well he or she is performing.
- Employ evaluation techniques that go up the hierarchy as well as down.
- Eliminate work/class distinctions (dress codes, lunchrooms, parking, perks, silly rules) that hamper creativity.
- Assure due process in grievance procedures.

If you can visualize the nature of a business in the future, the new organizational processes and practices necessary to make it work will follow. Many specialists now preach the gospel of worker empowerment. It is a rejection of the corporate hierarchy and paternalism of the past—and for good reason: empowerment increases energy. When workers are permitted to invest their energies in a personal process of learning and discovery while on the job, the increase in productivity, quality, and efficiency is phenomenal. Flattened management puts leaders closer to the customer and the worker. Employee ownership doubles the impact. More and more companies will be bought by employees, or at least will offer employees a stake in their success. Microsoft created so many millionaires through stock options that even the best programmers were willing to work long hours for low salaries if they had a piece of the future.

Power is energy, and it should expand as it flows through an organization. Energy contracts if power is concentrated at the top. Tight hierarchies hoard and constrict the flow of energy. Participative management expands decision-making power and energy. You can walk through the offices of most corporations and feel the difference. The headquarters of Mobil Oil is a high-rise steel fortress with frequent security checks between the street and the executive suites. Microsoft is a collection of low-rise buildings in a loose campus environment. Skilled, educated, and motivated workers can make decisions for themselves and they can be trusted. They don't require as many managers or bosses to guide or control them. Nordstrom has only one rule for employees: Use your good judgment in all situations. Everyone needs teachers and coaches, but the learning process is becoming more and more a dialogue of equals.

That sense of complexity and confusion and the feeling that we are reeling out of control are just signals that old operating frames and old realities are undergoing change. They are reminders of the deeper levels of transformation we are experiencing. They are not a new unsafe reality. Competence and flexibility will go a long way toward re-creating security. When you are secure, you reduce energy-stealing anxiety and increase self-confidence and optimism about the future.

Mastering New Forms of Intelligence

"All that is needed for a new universe is a new mind."

—William Carlos Williams

THE FUTURE WILL REQUIRE a higher and more socialized process of reasoning and more sophisticated reactions. We once believed that reason and logical analysis could solve all problems. A rational mind was all that we needed. In school, if we were good at narrow problem-solving we did well on IQ tests. High scores on aptitude tests made us believe that storing information—the kind that could be called up on demand—was the best use of the mind.

This old blueprint for intelligence may have served us reasonably well at one time. But not now, and not in the future. Now it limits our thinking. It leaves us aware only of the known, the understood, and the controllable. It suffocates fresh perceptions. It treats new information as just more data to be fed into well-established formulas of thought. Anything that doesn't fit is rejected. We are unaware of the subtle biases in our perception and thought.

We need a new vision of intelligence, one that integrates the right brain of images and creativity with the left brain of words and calculations, in the context of the social environment. You could call it "middle brain" intelligence, somewhere between reason and creative freefall. It is a fluid thought process that leads us to question our usual assumptions, to rein in our judgments, to take a fresh look at our world and what we really know about it. It is the core of a twenty-first-century mind and an essential skill for anyone who aspires to effective leadership.

Our brain has almost infinite capacity, the processing power of a hundred billion personal computers joined together. Yet even with that enormous capacity, too often we feel overloaded and we close down the system rather than learning to use our minds in new ways. Take a close look at a widely used aptitude test, the Scholastic Assessment Test (SAT), and you will get a better sense of how narrowly we define intelligence. The SAT *does* measure literacy, memory, vocabulary, general comprehension, pattern identification, spatial ability, reasoning, and math. But it *does not* measure many of the skills—actually, forms of intelligence—cataloged in this book. It doesn't, for example, measure perceptive ability, verbal communication skills, teamwork or relationship abilities, ingenuity, intuition, creativity, flexibility, mental health, multicultural awareness, varieties of experience, or ethical codes. Nor does it measure what is now being called emotional intelligence. If you come up with a creative answer or work out problems with a team, you flunk the SAT. The test favors homogenous groups with common experiences.

The SAT was developed in 1926, modeled after army tests from World War I, to measure the potential of the college-bound population. The baseline of "potential" in the 1920s was white, male, and agrarian/industrial. The SAT has been modified since then, but because of cost and standardization, no new baseline has been established. If you do well on the SAT, you may have the mind of a 1926 white guy from Massachusetts who would succeed as a World War I army officer. Your thinking and leadership skills are important and relevant, but may not be all that is needed to cope with our vastly different challenges today.

Not long ago, researchers examined the characteristics of students who won educational awards based on their performance on standardized tests such as the SAT. The study, done by an organization called FairTest, concluded that the same type of minds that could be found in college in 1920 are still being favored today.[1] Interestingly, many of these minds are now in the bodies of Asian Americans.

The anachronisms in the way we measure intelligence can also be found in IQ tests, which have not changed in any major way since the 1950s. In fact, they measure a very narrow range of intelligence. You don't have to understand the effect of your behavior on others or the environment. You can be a rabid racist or a psychopath planning your next murder and still get a high score on most IQ tests. You can be "intelligent" and run your corporation in a manner that exploits instead of supports the community. You can be a Mensa member with a very high IQ and not be able to hold a job or relate to anyone.

UNDERSTANDING WHO IS SMART

The debate over intelligence is a debate over higher standards. Over the past forty years, researchers of all kinds have uncovered the weaknesses of our tests and shown new respect for a broader-based definition of intelligence that reflects more than traditional fact retention and computation skills. Educators, in particular, are looking for a battery of tests that is more productive of real-world success. The designers of a school testing program in California, for example, put a premium on the skills required for "reasonably deciding what to think and do."[2] Among other things, students had to be able to determine the relevance of information, distinguish between fact and opinion, identify unstated assumptions, detect bias or propaganda, come up with reasonable alternatives or solutions, and predict possible consequences. Intelligence is the ability to make adaptive responses in new as well as old situations.

At Harvard, philosopher Nelson Goodman wanted to understand why some people were "creative" and others were not. In his work, Goodman expanded the concept of intelligence from "How smart is he or she?" to "*How* is he or she smart?" Motivation and interest in the task at hand—along with traits such as concentration, intention, purpose, drive, and tenacity—emerged as important influences.

Howard Gardner, a psychologist who helped to conduct this research, thought of intelligence as the ability to solve problems or create products. He devised the following list of eight primary forms of intelligence (to which I have added one of my own):[3]

1. Verbal/linguistic intelligence. This form of intelligence is revealed by a sensitivity to the meaning and order of words and the ability to make varied use of the language. Impromptu speaking, storytelling, humor, and joking are natural abilities associated with verbal/linguistic intelligence. So, too, is persuading someone to follow a course of action, or explaining, or teaching. Will Rogers had this form of intelligence. Good journalists also have it.

2. Logical/mathematical intelligence. This form of intelligence is easiest to standardize and measure. We usually refer to it as analytical or scientific thinking, and we see it in scientists, computer programmers, accountants, lawyers, bankers, and, of course, mathematicians, people who are problem solvers and consummate game players. They work with abstract symbols and are able to see

connections between pieces of information that others might miss. Einstein is one of the best examples of someone with this form of intelligence.

3. Visual/spatial intelligence. Persons with this form of intelligence are especially deft at conjuring up mental images and creating graphic representations. They are able to think in three-dimensional terms, to re-create the visual world. Picasso, whose paintings challenged our view of reality, was especially gifted at visualizing objects from different perspectives and angles. Besides painters and sculptors, this form of intelligence is found in designers and architects.

4. Body/kinesthetic intelligence. This form of intelligence makes possible the connections between mind and body that are necessary to succeed in activities such as dance, mime, sports, martial arts, and drama. Martha Graham and Michael Jordan delighted audiences with their explosive and sensitive uses of the body. Because they know how we move, inventors with this form of intelligence understand how to turn function into form. They intuitively feel what is possible in labor-saving devices and processes.

5. Musical/rhythmic intelligence. A person with this form of intelligence hears musical patterns and rhythms naturally and can reproduce them. It is an especially desirable form of intelligence because music has the capacity to alter our consciousness, reduce stress, and enhance brain function. For example, students who had just listened to Mozart scored higher on standard IQ tests than those who had spent the same period of time in meditation or silence. Researchers believe that the patterns in musical themes somehow prime the same neural network that the brain employs for complex visual-spatial tasks.

6. Interpersonal intelligence. Managers, counselors,

therapists, politicians, mediators, and human relations specialists display this form of intelligence. It is a must for workplace tasks such as negotiation and providing feedback or evaluation. Individuals with this form of intelligence have strong intuitive skills. They are especially able to read the moods, temperaments, motivations, and intentions of others. Abraham Lincoln, Mohandas Gandhi, and Martin Luther King, Jr., used interpersonal intelligence to change the world.

7. Intrapersonal intelligence. Sigmund Freud and Carl Jung demonstrated this form of intelligence, the ability to understand and articulate the inner workings of character and personality. The highest order of thinking and reasoning is present in a person who has intrapersonal intelligence. We often call it wisdom. He or she can see the larger picture and is open to the lure of the future. Within an organization, this ability is invaluable.

8. Spiritual intelligence. This form of intelligence is tentative; Gardner has yet to decide whether moral or spiritual intelligence qualifies for his list. It can be considered an amalgam of interpersonal and intrapersonal awareness with a "value" component added.

9. Practical intelligence. Gardner doesn't list this form of intelligence, but I do. It is the skill that enables some people to take a computer or clock apart and put it back together. I also think of practical intelligence as organizational intelligence or common sense, the ability to solve all sorts of daily problems without quite knowing how the solutions were reached. People with common sense may or may not test well, but they have a clear understanding of cause and effect. They use intelligence in combination with that understanding.

QUALITIES OF MIND

Rate yourself on each of these forms of intelligence. What are your strengths and weaknesses? How are they reflected in the kind of work you do and your relationships with others?

	Low				Moderate				High	
	1	2	3	4	5	6	7	8	9	10
1. Verbal/linguistic										
2. Logical/mathematical										
3. Visual/spatial										
4. Body/kinesthetic										
5. Musical/rhythmic										
6. Interpersonal										
7. Intrapersonal										
8. Spiritual										
9. Practical										

Don't let this list intimidate you. There is increasingly strong evidence that intelligence can be taught, despite ongoing arguments about genetic predetermination. Also, the levels of each of these forms of intelligence can vary from one person to the next. Albert Einstein had a high degree of logical and spatial intelligence, but his lack of personal skills was legendary. He left those details to others.

Regardless of the forms of our intelligence, we also need to know how we think. Researcher Geil Browning studies approaches to problem solving.[4] She identifies four "styles" that people use to process information: analytical, conceptual, structural, and social. She concludes that most of us use more than one of them, depending on the problem before us. Her work helps us visualize thought processes, something that makes communication and negotiation easier. When forming a creative and productive team for problem solving or futuring consider combining different thinking styles.

Analytical thinkers are the most logical. They must have facts, figures, directions and reasons to approach problem solving. They want to design a system. They see themselves as straightforward, clear and purposeful. In a team meeting they ask, "Is this feasible?"

Conceptual thinkers accept information in almost any form. They enjoy a challenge and often plunge into the problem-solving process before considering what direction to take. They want to paint a picture. They don't mind mistakes. They usually suggest, "Let's look at this problem in a different way."

Structural thinkers draw comparisons and look for systematic links to determine the source of a problem. They prefer creating flow charts. They organize the components of the problem and the possible solutions and ask, "How does this apply to our situation?"

Social thinkers are the facilitators of group process. They talk to everyone; they weigh all the solutions equally; they may identify the best solution but not know how they reached it. In a team situation they ask, "What do you think of this idea?"

Review these four styles and combine them with the nine forms of intelligence outlined on pages 182 through 184. Try to identify yourself and imagine how different problems or situations engage different aspects of your intelligence or thinking style. Create a perfect team for a problem you are currently trying to solve. What ideal set of minds would potentially be the most intelligent and the best at processing?

British researcher Edward De Bono, in a series of books on intelligence, believes he has the answer. He adds the term *lateral thinking* to this mix. He sees it as the most productive thinking process because it is easily taught and allows everyone in a group, regardless of their intelligence frame or thinking style, to operate with the same broad set of thinking tools.

Lateral thinking is similar to what others currently call critical or system thinking. It enables us to view a problem from all sides and understand all the alternatives before devising a solution. It requires us to abandon certainty and security, at least for the moment. De Bono's most useful exercise in lateral thinking is called PMI, an acronym for Plus, Minus, and Interesting.[5] Participants are divided into small groups and are asked to evaluate what is good (plus), what is bad (minus), and what is interesting about an idea. In a session with a group of auto manufacturers, for example, De Bono posed the suggestion that all cars should be painted yellow. Here is how the group reacted:

Good (Plus)	Bad (Minus)	Interesting
• Easier to see on the roads.	• Boring.	• Interesting to see if different shades of yellow arose.
• Easier to see at night.	• Difficult to recognize your car.	
• No problem in deciding which color you want.	• Very difficult to find your car in a parking lot.	• Interesting to see if people appreciated the safety factor.
• No waiting to get the color you want.	• Easier to steal cars.	• Interesting to see whether attitudes toward cars changed.
• Easier for the manufacturer.	• The abundance of yellow might tire the eyes.	
• The dealer would need less stock.	• Car chases would be difficult for the police.	• Interesting to see if trim acquired a different color.
• It might take the "macho" element out of car ownership.	• Accident witnesses would have a harder time.	• Interesting to see if this were enforceable.
• Cars would tend to become transport items.	• Restriction of your freedom to choose.	• Interesting to see who would support the suggestion.
• In minor collisions the paint rubbed off onto your car would be the same color.	• Some paint companies might go out of business.	

Exercises in lateral thinking work best if each category (good, bad, and interesting) is considered separately and in order when pondering an idea or a problem rather

than brainstorming them in the random fashion preferred by conceptual thinkers. Such exercises can be particularly useful when you are floating some new idea
about your business or looking for a solution to some
problem. They help people focus their perceptions and
articulate their reactions and responses. *Common Ground,*
a PBS series designed to bring opposing sides together on
several controversial issues, used lateral thinking with
powerful results. Participants were able to put aside
rhetoric and emotion and find they had far more in common than they realized.

PUTTING IT ALL TOGETHER

We are all, to one degree or another, system thinkers. (I
prefer the term *system thinking* to De Bono's *lateral thinking* because we are looking at the whole to understand
the parts.) We must also combine disparate parts into coherent wholes to put together the puzzles and solve the
problems of daily life. A system thinker believes in cooperation and knows that pooling or combining ideas,
skills, and experience improves innovation, efficiency,
and performance. I think of system thinking as broad-
scope intelligence and very much like synergy, a buzz-
word in business in the 1990s. Companies that practiced
synergy did so by buying or developing related businesses or by welding their existing units into a more coherent whole.

Social scientists used system thinking in the 1970s
when they began working together to examine the "culture of poverty" as a whole. Edward Demming used it to
fine-tune quality processes. The earliest ideas about man
and environment as a whole organism represented system thinking. The interrelationship of mind and body in
the healing process is another example. When we think
about parts of a system, separate from the whole, we cut
ourselves off from important information.

System thinking can bridge the gap that sometimes exists between reality and our perception of reality. For example, unproductive workers, falling orders, and sagging profits are indicators of serious problems in any business. Our usual way of thinking may cause us to look at each in isolation. But system thinking helps us understand that all parts of a business or a process are connected, and that when one part is challenged, all the others are as well. We may look for productivity problems on the production line and create new incentives if salespeople are not doing well, but the real "cause" of our problems may be hidden in the system that underlies the entire enterprise. System thinking accepts the interrelatedness of all things. System thinking is usually the best way to find out what is going on.

System thinking can help all of us understand the zigzag of change. It enables us to see the big picture. From that vantage point we can more easily perceive the changing realities of our work and lives and solve problems. Here are some of the basic characteristics of a system thinker:

- You are physically and intellectually alert.
- You are always wondering how things can be improved.
- You are able to resolve conflict by agreeing to disagree on some points and moving the discussion forward.
- You do not demand perfection from yourself or others.
- You are imaginative and creative.
- You are empathetic and compassionate.
- You are comfortable with chaos.
- You are a nonconformist in one way or another.
- You have a sense of humor.

THINKING SKILLS

We can learn to be skilled thinkers. We also can learn to think about the thinking process, something that we seldom do. We always assume that *we*, at least, are intelligent and open-minded. We don't observe ourselves as closely as we do others. With that in mind, here are some exercises to help develop skilled thinking:

Evaluate and Identify Your Thinking

Athletes and dancers are taught to think about their every move. Like them, all of us need to develop the ability to stand back and evaluate how we think, even as we are thinking. Do you hit blank spots or moments when you become emotional? Do you have difficulty getting started or feel that your alternatives are hopelessly limited? Are you sometimes frustrated by a lack of creativity or by the same old ideas repeating themselves? Do you have an odd way of looking at things? Do you sometimes jump to conclusions? Work your way through a checklist like this—one that you create—and you are thinking about thinking.

In a meeting or conversation, see if you can analyze the thinking processes being used by other people. When you are wrestling with a decision, try to be aware of how your mind is working. See if you can visualize the thinking you are using to solve a problem. Work on knowing the type of thinking necessary to accomplish a task. Be genuinely focused. Thinking about thinking is hard at first, but it eventually becomes second nature.

Use De Bono's Hats

Edward De Bono helps us visualize the various ways in which people think by relating them to imaginary hats they are wearing. Here is a condensed version of his guide:[6]

White hat—the white-hat thinker is mainly concerned with facts and figures.

Red hat—the red-hat thinker operates from an emotional stance.

Black hat—the black-hat thinker dwells on why something cannot be done.

Yellow hat—the yellow-hat thinker is optimistic.

Green hat—the green-hat thinker is creative and open to new ideas.

Blue hat—the blue-hat thinker is concerned with control.

Try "wearing" some of these different hats when you are confronted with a problem. Organize a group to argue solutions from each of these points of view. It will help you understand how other people think. Try reacting to a new idea from the points of view of different people in your organization or corporation. Become a customer, client, line worker, supervisor, executive, or board member. How does position change your point of view? Does position actually change your thinking process?

Create Alternatives

We resist examining alternatives because that can lead to confusion or ambivalence. Americans often prefer extremes to ambivalence. Many workers prefer a manager who will quickly diagnose a problem and issue directions for solving it. A manager who reviews all the data, considers a number of alternatives, makes tentative statements, and withholds a final judgment may seem indecisive.

One who seeks the workers' opinions or a team consensus might seem unsure. Yet, much of the conflict surrounding the problems we face in the workforce, the country, or the community stems from a lack of willingness to consider alternatives seriously. Asking questions about alternatives seems common sense, but it is rarely done in a disciplined and open manner. Political expediency and old myths about leadership get in the way.

Step Outside the Usual

Outward Bound and other team-building exercises use unusual games and challenges that encourage participants to search for creative alternatives. In one exercise I watched at BellSouth, each team was given two two-by-fours with rope handles and told to cross an imaginary river. The obvious solution was also the most physically demanding: to line up team members in single file with their left feet on one board and their right feet on the other, then use the rope handles to lift and move the boards forward like cross-country skis. The team that had chosen athletic members whizzed across. They then pushed the boards back over the imaginary gap so that other members of their team could cross. A second team, which lacked the athletic skill of the first, came up with a different solution: to lay the boards end to end, borrowing one extra board from a third team that figured it would otherwise lose out. All their team members simply walked across on a one-board-wide "bridge," keeping their balance by holding hands. They beat the first team's time by a wide margin and left a bridge behind that the third team used.

When we develop the ability to generate alternatives no matter what the situation, we are in control of the thinking process. Remember this old adage: "When you are up to your ass in alligators, it's hard to remember that the objective was to drain the swamp." When you actually go through the process of looking for and thinking about all the ways to look at a situation, you will see the alligators *before* you wade into the swamp.

Make Sure You Know What the Problem Is

We often put too much energy into solving the wrong problem. Sometimes we believe workers are the problem when it is management. Or we think it is someone else's behavior when it is our own. Or we try to apply logic to solve a problem that has more to do with tradition or privilege. We think, for example, that a good plan is all we need to solve the health-care problem of the nineties, when, in fact, it may require a fundamental change in beliefs about health-care professionals and life and death values.

Try this exercise. In a group discussion, ask people to write down what seems to be an agreed-upon problem. Then ask them to go one level deeper and individually reflect on whether there is something else that might be the real problem. Have them write down their conclusions and reopen the discussion. A problem that has an obvious cause is usually not much of a problem.

Use a Flow Analysis of Situations

Ask questions about things that are going on in your life and your business to see how they can be improved. Looking critically at things that are not currently problems is a great way to make sure they don't become problems. Be willing to challenge your own assumptions. Ask friends and colleagues if they agree with your assessments. If we are stunned by a business or a relationship failure, it is because we were badly detached from what was happening and avoided continuous evaluation.

Be Humble

There can be a direct relationship between humility and intelligence. The higher the level of humility, the higher the intelligence. Humility keeps us open. Humiliation is an excellent teacher whether it is forced upon us or is self-generated. Arrogance does just the reverse. Believing that your way of thinking is the only way is a form of arrogance. How many companies have dropped from sight because an arrogant mind-set blinded them to changing realities?

History provides useful examples. America's victory over the Japanese in World War II was a source of great humiliation for the people of Japan. But the war experience also opened up many Japanese minds to the usefulness of Western technology and marketing, and they quickly became a formidable production and export machine. In turn, the Japanese eventually humbled American businesses through higher quality production standards. We gradually responded with changes in the way we market, manufacture, and think about products and services. Humility, whether it is a result of failure or competition, makes us recognize the need to change the way we think.

Think About Your Experiences

Can you remember trying to solve a problem but not pursuing alternatives until someone or something hit you over the head? Why do you think that happened? Was there a failure of perspective? Did old myths and traditions cloud your deliberation process? Were you reluctant to face the possibility of change? Try to find the answers to these questions by reviewing some of your experiences with problem solving. Use this list to ask yourself:

> Is my instinct to search for alternatives strong
>   enough that I will do it even if there is no al-
>   ternative in sight?
> Am I willing to listen to the ideas of others and

show interest in other people's solutions? Do
I avoid nitpicking?

Do I refuse to get caught up in negative thinking and reduce debate to personal attacks?

Do I understand the importance of emotions,
feelings, and values in thinking, but avoid letting them derail or overpower the process?

Consider EQ

The most exciting breakthroughs in the next century
may not be in technology but in our concepts of what it
means to be a human. New brain research suggests that
emotional intelligence, or emotional quotient (EQ), not
IQ, may be the truest predictor of success. EQ is a combination of Gardner's intrapersonal and interpersonal
qualities of mind. Psychoanalyst Erik Erikson described it
as the ability to successfully integrate the many facets of
a personality, and called it "ego integrity." Too many of us
let emotions drive our thought processes while we discount the emotions of others. Researchers generally
agree that traditional IQ counts for only about 20 percent
of success. The rest depends on the advantages derived
from class, luck, character, personality, and cultural
awareness.

To test your EQ, ask yourself these questions:

How smart are you about how you or others
feel?

How often are you surprised?

Can you sense the mood of a group you are
speaking to?

Are you optimistic? (Psychologist Martin Seligman cites optimism as the most accurate
measure of EQ.)

BARRIERS TO THINKING

There are all sorts of barriers that can impede the way we think about problems or change. They are not matters of stupidity or pathology. Rather, they arise from the way the mind handles information. Here is a sampler of barriers to thinking:

Absolutes

People who think in absolutes usually don't listen to anyone but themselves. They resist new ideas and try to preserve the status quo. I call this "rock logic." Beware of anybody who says, "There is only one right way." Be willing to admit that you don't know, be willing to suspend judgment. People who think they know usually stopped thinking long ago.

Contentment

Those who are content see no reason to change. "If it ain't broke, don't fix it." This kind of resistance to change is understandable. At a certain age, the future looks far less promising than the present. If you have made your fortune or settled into a certain lifestyle, you may have no interest in thinking about alternatives. If you want to preserve your comfortable place in a particular corporate or social niche—the one that let you in, regardless of whom it shut out—then thinking may be a threat to your sense of self and your peace of mind. On the other hand, discomfort and discontent are powerful motivators for thinking about change.

Immediate Gratification

This is a characteristic of our age, from the credit card that replaced layaway to the remote control that made channel surfing our favorite form of exercise. In the business world, many companies have come to think mainly in terms of quarterly performance and the bottom line, not research and development and the products of the future. Managing by best-sellers is a sure sign that businesses are not thinking for themselves, even though greater profits may lie in systematically examining the collective mind of their companies.

At home, television has wrought changes in our thought processes that we have yet to comprehend. I was ten when our first TV arrived. We had a family portrait taken with the set as a centerpiece. TV immediately began to whittle away our imaging skills, our imaginations, and our ability to think for ourselves. We didn't have to create the pictures. TV provided sensory stimulation and mindless diversion.

Why does this matter? Because once we begin to lose our ability to imagine or create, we cannot envision the future. Readers, for example, create images in their minds from the print on a page. It is an important thinking process that television eliminates. The present, with its multiple diversions and options, becomes so overwhelming that the motivation to plan or to act seems to slip away. For some who watch television, it becomes difficult for their minds to think ahead, and their values shift accordingly.

But television also connects us to worlds we might not otherwise know or see. It creates national media experiences—whether the funeral of a president, the Anita Hill/Clarence Thomas hearings, or the O. J. Simpson trial—that operate as civic dramas and lessons. Television teaches and reveals who we are. It generates national conversations. It is such a young medium that we have yet to learn, as we ultimately did with the printing press, how to use it to best serve the public interest.

Polarity Thinking

With polarity thinkers, it is either/or. There is no in between. Polarity thinking stops dialogue. It freezes people into place and leads them to ignore data that supports other positions until change is forced upon them by failure or crisis. I have seen a particular kind of polarity thinking in troubled companies. Executives in search of a more effective management style often bounce from one extreme to another. They trade all the weaknesses of a "controlling" style for what they think are all the strengths of a "flexible/open" approach to management. What they too often get are the weaknesses of the new style while losing the strengths of the old.

Being Too Smart

Highly intelligent people sometimes make up their minds so quickly that they overlook critical flaws in the process. Their minds are like computers that can sift vast amounts of data with few signals, but they often fail to consider elements that should be factors in their decisions and, in particular, the consequences of their decisions. This is where someone who thinks more slowly can have an unexpected advantage. That person may follow a more careful thinking process—taking in more signals, especially social responses, weighing all the elements involved, noticing where data is missing or spotting paths of inquiry that have not been taken, considering consequences. It may take them longer to reach a conclusion, but their decisions are usually more firmly based on the realities of a situation.

Wishful Thinking, Mindless Conformity, and Simplistic Thinking

Images generated by our electronic media have contributed to the prevalence of these thought processes. TV commercials, in particular, are aimed at wishful thinkers who are easily convinced that some product will change their lives. Commercials sell easy sex, instant self-confidence, and financial schemes to make you rich. On the sitcoms, the "beautiful people" never seem to work. Wishful thinkers are seldom doers. As a result, their thought processes become ever more simple and visceral as life becomes ever more complex.

Mindless conformity shows up in corporations and organizations that have a lodge mentality. The same is true of social groups. Once an individual decides that his or her gang is superior, the brain focuses only on who is "one of us" and who isn't—and what has to be done, worn, or owned to make that distinction clear. Many companies still have severe dress codes, time-consuming rituals, and elaborate rules that control the flow of information. When a manager is overly concerned about the meaning of your facial hair, talks about the "chain of command," or tells you to "go by the rules," you can assume that only a very small part of his creative brain is working.

Rituals and conformity can be useful in times of economic stability. They allow an organization to create bonds and feelings of solidarity. But in times of change, the rigidity of the simplistic thinking they encourage makes it impossible for the group to pick up the signals of change and envision the future.

Out of the Gut

Gut responses may be critical when you are confronted by a mountain lion or a bull. Such instinctual responses enabled our ancestors to survive. But in other situations, we need to be wary of what our gut is telling us. It may be signaling real danger—or it may be transmitting old and not very useful ways of thinking or responding. Evolutionary biologists believe that neural pathways develop over millions of years. What happens when they suddenly become maladaptive? One of the dangers of television and film violence is its reenforcement of these old response pathways. If you are not sickened viscerally by gratuitous violence, if you internally cheer it on or feel your fist clench in a fight response, your gut is out-of-date. If "fight or flight" is your only set of alternatives when confronting conflict, even in business, you are not thinking. Instincts can give us important information about what to do, or they can be "knee jerks" from the past that limit our ability to assess the present.

Gut responses also enable us to deny problems or put the blame or responsibility on others because it feels right. The most important question to ask yourself when facing any conflict or problem is "What part did I play in this?" You need to know how to suspend your gut responses until all the data are in.

Gender

Our world is gradually giving way to a more androgynous view of the way we think. A revolution is going on around gender in the thinking processes, just as it is in our lives and work. Psychology is now studying the underutilized and, in many ways, "feminine" aspects of our thought processes: subjectivity, cooperation, relatedness, and intuition. Biology has turned its interest toward symbiosis, physics is probing quantum mechanics, mathematics is finding comfort in chaos theory, and computer whizzes talk easily about fuzzy logic. Likewise, the once-rigid boundaries that separated "masculine" and "feminine" thought processes are beginning to blur and may one day disappear completely. In view of that prospect, it makes less and less sense to allow our thought processes to be dominated by gender stereotypes, what is believed to be typically male or female. Whatever the future brings, the fewer barriers to thinking we have to surmount, the more responsive we are to change.

FUTURE SKILLS

Any manager of a company or other organization is naturally concerned about the future. That manager's success can depend on his or her ability to understand what is coming in technology, economics, demographics, culture, and lifestyles. Yet we live in a time when people seem more intimidated by the future than ever before. Ian Morrison, author of *Future Tense* and president of the Institute for the Future in Menlo Park, California, calls this the "age of insecurity," especially among babyboomers, who are facing the uncertainties of middle age as well as of the future.[7]

Morrison's antidote is a set of three tools with which to explore the future: *scenarios*, plausible stories about the future; *forecasts*, likely stories about the future; and *wild cards*, low-probability, high-impact future trends and events. Using the guide that follows, set aside some time each week, at home or at work, to think five years down the line.

Scenarios

Begin this exercise by identifying the critical issues that your company or organization is facing now or will probably have to face in the future. Next, identify the force or trends behind each issue. For example, the babyboomers are aging, and that force will drive many marketing trends. Women in the workplace are an important force; outsourcing is another major trend. Now generate probable scenarios around the two or three issues that seem most important to your business. Morrison suggests doing this by asking what might cause current forces or trends to falter or reverse themselves.

What, for example, might happen if a new diet stretched life spans to one hundred years? How might people change their work and consumption habits? Could declining fertility, linked to workforce tension, persuade women to return home? How would the in-creasing number of househusbands affect lifestyles and patterns of consumption? How much work will be done from technological cottages?

In constructing your scenario, go to outside experts and clients and ask for their input. Talk to someone who is part of the trend you are examining. How many octogenarians still want to work, how many women who have returned home are satisfied, how many househusbands believe that the lifestyle is right for them? Can you measure the strength and the perma-nence of a trend? What more do you need to know? If you can confirm the strength of the trend now, how can you and your company position yourselves to take ad-vantage of it?

Forecasts

Here, you are going to narrow down your scenarios to one forecast that you might be willing to bet the store on. Given what you know about yourself or your com-pany and the strength of a trend, what is your single most promising shot? Challenge the conventional as-sumptions. Ask tougher, more penetrating questions about what is going on. If we weren't already doing this today, would we start doing it tomorrow? This is the time to stampede all the sacred cows. Think about breaking the rules. Consider unconventional ideas, products, or services.

See, for example, how this approach played out with the issue of health-care costs. The assumption that employers were worried most about soaring costs caused insurers to scramble to develop new system limits. But they turned out to be a hard sell. In-depth interviews of employers produced the explanation: The employers were not as concerned about health-care costs, which by then were stabilizing with the advent of managed care, as they were about other government-imposed costs such as Workmen's Compensation. When entry-level

employees were asked their concerns about future benefits, they put day care for their children and grandchildren near the top of the list, along with health care.
Older employees put elder care near the top of theirs.
Men as well as women in management were concerned
about the stress they felt from trying to balance work demands with their commitment to their children.

You can learn much from your customers or clients,
but don't expect them to lead you. Customers didn't demand cellular telephones, fax machines, minivans, or
CDs. They didn't want to pump their own gas and they
didn't imagine ATMs and twenty-four-hour help lines.
The best new products and services don't exist now, and
you may have a whole new set of customers by the year
2000.

Take time to think about the future. Most of my corporate clients can discuss topics such as sales targets, executive compensation, overhead, and prices for days, but
they have much less to say about the implications of
market trends. They just don't devote enough time to
understanding the forces shaping the future of their
companies. To stimulate that kind of thought and understanding, managers can ask themselves the following
questions about any trend under consideration:

How might this trend influence our current cus-
   tomers?
How might it influence our current core busi-
   ness?
How might it create new customers?
Who are the potential customers?
What are our two closest competitors doing
   about this trend?
What other trends might be coevolving with
   this one?
How fast is this trend developing and what
   might accelerate it or slow it down?
What are the risks of committing to this trend?
   What are the rewards?

Get your information on trends to everyone else in your company as fast as possible. Condense it, simplify it, make it interesting and readable, and share it on a regular basis. Drop the idea that only a few people need to know what is "in the works." Opening up the discussion will generate potentially valuable feedback that otherwise remains bottled up.

Wal-Mart managers at every level get together in regional groups once a week to exchange information about competitors, customers, successes, and failures. Their data is anecdotal and intuitive but it is current and on the cutting edge.

Forecasting trends, like weather forecasting, will never become an exact science. There are too many variables. But the more information you can gather, the more ideas you can generate, and the greater the variety of thinking you can bring to the process, the more likely it is that your predictions will be accurate.

Wild Cards

Thinking about wild cards, "what-ifs," is one way of handling uncertainties in a scenario or a forecast. Wild cards are possible discontinuities, surprises. Morrison describes them as "something that would scare the hell out of the CEO."

- What if internal combustion engines were banned from city streets?
- What if the exchange of cash was eliminated completely from all our transactions?
- What if your product or service was declared illegal or suddenly became obsolete?
- What if the corporate headquarters or main manufacturing center burned down? Would you rebuild?
- What if birth control implants became available for men?

- What if skin color could be lightened in "blanding" booths?
- What if animals began to communicate through brain wave synthesizers?
- What if a worldwide workweek of twenty-five hours became the norm?
- What if the environmental movement was stopped?

Global warming, concern about asbestos as a carcinogen, children sniffing glue, breast implants, and secondhand smoke—all of these were wild cards that have affected the fortunes of the involved industries. Contrarians such as Ted Turner (CNN) and Anita Roddick (Body Shop) deal wild cards; they can change an industry seemingly overnight. What wild cards could impact you and your company? Thinking about wild cards will expose both your strengths and your vulnerabilities.

Two hundred and thirty of the Fortune 500 companies dropped off the list between 1985 and 1995. Imagine it is the year 2010 and your company, industry, or organization is gone. Do you know why? Did you see it coming? If not, why not? What could you have done to stay in business? When I asked American Heart Association executives what their organization might look like in the year 2000, the room divided into pessimists and optimists. The pessimists talked about the loss of volunteers (no one has time), competition (HMOs), and management problems. The optimists created the International Heart Association and then combined all the "individual organ" associations into the Global Body Group.

Logic alone is insufficient to achieve the best resolution of many of our problems. The future challenges us to question our own minds and how we think, to reexamine our assumptions and see how they connect to the changing realities of our world. Thinking must become a more fluid process; I call it "water logic" because the future will require the development of a fluid, more adaptive level of reaction and response. As humanity evolves, creating ever more complex patterns, the ability to understand, synthesize, and adapt to those patterns will become basic intelligence.

SKILL 8

Profiting from Diversity

"From genetics we have learned that hybrids typically grow faster, are larger, are more fertile, show greater disease resistance, and are in general better at adapting to their environments. From history and political sciences, we learned that monolithic structures are less stable and perish long before pluralistic governments with competitive subgroups fail. From education we know that the development of social skills and personal growth are superior in integrated settings. It therefore seems logical that successful leadership and management of groups composed of men and women from several cultural groups will lead to continued existence and possible improvements in long-term productivity and effectiveness."

—V. ROBERT HAYLES, OFFICE OF NAVAL RESEARCH,
ARLINGTON, VIRGINIA

A WORLD MARKETPLACE FOR OUR products and our services comes with this requirement: that we make ourselves into global citizens, able to move easily among countries, currencies, languages, and customs. Global citizens are comfortable living and doing business anywhere. This new requirement for cultural sensitivity is not something that only Americans are grappling with. Other nations have their antennae out for us just as we have ours out for them. We are all sniffing around this new world.

Record numbers of American businesses are opening up new territory from Prague to Ho Chi Minh City to Beijing. Other countries still send their brightest young people here for a good education, after which they, more often than in the past, head home for opportunity. This global economic embrace requires us to be at ease with diversity. Our ability to come to terms with differences in nationality, race, ethnicity, gender, disability, and religion—all the elements of diversity—will be a critical predictor of economic success in the next century.

By coming to terms with diversity, I mean something more than treating others with fairness and equality. Diversity suggests that the "irregulars"—people who are not like us—have skills that we "regulars" might actually need and eventually want. We learn to value their ideas. I call it culture-free learning, or shaking off the limits of one culture. When business realizes diversity can add value, old beliefs about "them" start to become irrelevant. Diversity translates into clients and customers. Diversity promises an organization competitive advantage.

Organizations with "high diversity IQs" are able to draw on a world brain pool, a rich mix of thinking and perceptions. They are more responsive and more flexible, make smarter decisions, and are especially creative at problem solving. They hire from a much larger talent pool, and they have a better understanding of their customers. Consultant Jon Katzenbach researched top change agents and found them to be mavericks, "funny little fat guys with thick glasses"—and more often women.[1] Companies such as General Electric and Coca-Cola can recognize talent and profit from diversity. In their overseas operations, both hire local managers who know what their communities prefer and how to market and distribute a product without offending local customs. Work assignments are rotated so that foreign employees have experience in North America and American employees spend time abroad.

When GE designed appliances for the European market, it included Europeans on the design teams. The products that resulted took into account customer preference for smaller appliances with fewer options and made GE competitive with German and French manufacturers. GE avoided the missteps of American auto manufacturers in Japan, whose products until recently largely ignored the preferences of Japanese auto buyers. Coca-Cola also does a good job of listening to ideas from its international workforce. When employees in Japan suggested cold coffee in cans might be a hit in their country, Coca-Cola acted on the idea.

Executives whose lives have included diversity experiences find themselves well prepared for the risks of international business. American Seafoods is a primarily Norwegian-owned company based in Seattle, Vladivostok, and Buenos Aires. Its executive for a number of years was Carl Mundt, a German-Irish maritime attorney from Seattle whose father had worked in Uruguay and Argentina. Mundt speaks fluent Spanish. When fishing restrictions limited access to the Bering Sea, he opened a trawler operation in waters off Argentina. His boats tripled the length of their season and avoided the bankruptcy faced by other companies.

Ted Evans runs a seafood quality and inspection company, Surefish, that maintains laboratories all over the world. Evans was raised in Wisconsin by parents who took in foreign exchange students. He served in Vietnam, trained as a marine attorney, and worked for United States and United Nations agencies dealing with ocean resources. He travels easily through shrimp-processing plants in Thailand, crab-processing plants in China, surimi and squid plants in Japan, and frozen-fish warehouses in Seattle.

Both Mundt and Evans had diversity experiences starting in childhood, and broadened them as adults through business, friendships, and travel. Managers like these are valuable assets because they notice new clients or customers and new opportunities. In contrast, American life insurance and financial management companies seem unable to see the diverse markets in their own country, let alone those abroad. I asked groups of "wealth transfer" specialists about their minority or ethnic clients in 1995. Only one had a non-Caucasian client. None of the others was seeking such clients.

Ironically, there was a time when overseas experience was something that most managers tried to avoid. The bias against promoting managers from foreign divisions was so pronounced that such assignments were perceived as career killers. Now that bias is being replaced by a recognition that foreign experience sets an employee apart from the clutch of MBAs coveting the same job. In many companies today, overseas experience is virtually essential for promotion to top management. American corporations, in fact, are increasing their overseas executive staffing faster than their domestic executives. Expatriate executives who chose to live their lives in another country are increasingly being courted by companies looking for someone who already knows the culture and market they hope to penetrate. They want international citizens who can hit the ground running.

Europeans are even more sensitive to this. That's one reason, for example, why the Germans are more successful than Americans in selling auto parts to the Japanese and why the British are still more successful bankers than Americans in Asia.

Here is a way to measure your diversity experience. What elements of other cultures touch upon your life every day? How often do you spend work or personal time with individuals from different groups? Go down this list of possible contacts with other racial, ethnic, religious, national, and gender groups and rate your experiences on a 1-to-10 scale.

Business contacts
Business partners
Working closely to-
   gether
Working in the
   same general
   area

Attend meetings,
   conferences
Travel in the same
   vehicle
Eat together
Mentor or super-
   vise

Train
Use as professionals
in your personal
life (dentist, doc-
tor, lawyer, ac-
countant, stylist,
housekeeper,
pharmacist,
physical trainer,
dry cleaner,
counselor, minis-
ter, teacher)
Casual social
events (parties,
large dinners,
clubs, golf)
On sports team to-
gether
Children play with

Children attend
school with
Children's friends
Your friends
Invite to your
home, accept in-
vitations to their
home
Go dancing to-
gether
Vacation together
Live in the same
neighborhood
Attend the same
church
Read their litera-
ture
Eat their food
Listen to their
music

Now think of ways to broaden your diversity experience. When you cannot do it in the routine of business,
do it in your personal life. Join community groups that
have a diverse membership. Check out the films, read
the books, and listen to the music of other groups. Travel.

A MULTICULTURAL WORKFORCE

In a *New York Times* interview, Marian Stetson-Rodriguez,
president of LinguaTec Inc., described work teams in Silicon Valley: "You can go into a company around here
nowadays and find people from Tonga, South Korea and
Romania working side by side. But even appearances
can be confusing. We have people who look African-
American but are from Somalia or Suriname. I know of
one manager who looks Chinese and has a Chinese

name, but speaks perfect English and comes from Argentina."[2]

The Western workforce of the past—structured largely around able-bodied white males—is transforming itself into one of almost unimaginable diversity. I created a lecture series titled "Hire the One with the Turban" just to make this point, and was startled when people began to ask me what the quota for Sikhs was. I had only hoped to create a global awareness, not a new minority. The worldwide migration of professionals, so visible in the Silicon Valley, is an important force behind this change. But it is mainly being driven by broad shifts in the American population. Demographers estimate that by the year 2050, more than 60 percent of the U.S. workforce will be people of color and more than 40 percent will be female.[3]

Progress toward a multicultural workforce in this country has been slow. Only when affirmative action was mandated by law in the 1960s did businesses, universities, and government agencies assume—some more willingly than others—the responsibility of overcoming centuries of racial and sexual discrimination. At first, any suggestions of real skills among the minorities were limited. Baseball had disproved this theory in 1947 with Jackie Robinson, but in football, when African Americans finally began to play quarterback, there were comments such as "Well, they still don't have the coach part in their brain." When African Americans became successful coaches, more than one commentator remarked, "Well, they are still not smart enough to be general managers."

At each new skill level, minorities find that they must prove their competence. When enough skills are demonstrated and are recognized, the majority begins to see the pragmatic value of diversity. But the process can take a long time. In corporate America, for example, 96 percent of senior executive positions are still held by white males. *Fortune* magazine estimates that "white men are in no danger of losing or even sharing control of management for at least 25 years at current rates of change."[4]

When the "regulars" are asked or required to make room for those they consider "irregulars," it hurts. For too many the basic whine remains: "Equality is fine, I'm all for it, as long as I don't have to give up my advantages and privileges." The impact on lives and legacies can be profound. In medical schools, for example, female and minority admissions have risen from 7 percent to 47 percent in just twenty years.[5] It has appeared, to some, as if they were victims of "reverse discrimination."

The white son of a physician whose father was himself the son of a physician is angry to discover that his application to medical school has been rejected. The standards have not been lowered to admit the "others;" it's just that there is more competition. The old connections don't work as they used to, and a family legacy is shattered. There are many new professions open to the young man—gene research, astrophysics, fiber optics—but none is going to assuage his grief if he had his heart set on being a physician just like his dad.

It is worse for those who are unemployed or losing ground in this new world. They suspect that people who are different or new are somehow to blame, and they create scapegoats. The situation triggers a "territorial imperative"—almost a cell-level response—deep in our survival tool kit. Feeling entitled to and fighting for territory are so much a part of our unconscious memory that racial, ethnic, and national groups all over the world battle each other to the death to retain their privileges and their pieces of turf.

Today it may seem easier to be a woman and see your horizons expanding even beyond your dreams than to be a man whose traditional expectations are being challenged. There is always a struggle when "new arrivals" seek to gain economic status and political power. Women have every right to pursue equality, but all of us must be aware of the losses, psychic and economic, that some white males perceive or endure. This struggle has gone on throughout our history because no other nation has made diversity a cornerstone of its existence and its constitution. At one time or another most Americans were "new arrivals" making new demands. The Japanese require their citizens to be of Japanese descent and find it hard to assimilate anyone else. We welcome everyone. When we feel threatened by new arrivals or the illusions we hold about them, we often talk about changing our immigration policy. But it is more than a policy. It is our national identity and our unifying creed: *E pluribus unum*—"Out of the many, one."

Where other nations have a whole culture based on a single language or group of dialects, we have many Americans for whom English is a second language. Where other cultures have a shared genetic pool, we have the most tangled genetic pool the world has ever known. We have no national dress, dance, music, or religion. Our culture is, by its very nature, one of diversity. We are one nation of many cultures. We are, in fact, a precursor of what lies ahead—one world of many cultures. How well we accommodate diversity is indicative of how well we will handle future change. We are engaged, writes essayist Asta Bowen, in a pioneer effort to "tune democracy to its finest tolerance."[6]

RACE AND ETHNICITY MYTHS

Much of what we now fight about in the race and ethnicity "wars" will soon be irrelevant. Racial categories on census forms are becoming useless because of the genetic absurdity of categories such as "Hispanic," "African-American," or "Asian." Many groups with a common label no longer have a common gene pool, if they ever did. Census officials are considering new categories such as "biracial" or "multiracial." "Other" already exists. Put simply, racial and ethnic prejudices are increasingly irrational and dependent on myths and stereotypes. At some point not too distant, it will be hard to know whom to hate.

The myth of a genetic base for even the most basic racial categories has been exploded by recent research. *The History and Geography of Human Genes*, by Paola Menozzi and Alberta Piazza (1995), is a genetic atlas of the world based on the analysis of blood from gene pools in place in 1500, before explorers opened the "New World."[7] Their findings essentially eliminate the racial category of Caucasian. Most Europeans are a combination of 65 percent Asian and 35 percent African when blood, not myth, is the measure. This is a classic example of technology (gene research) pushing consciousness and perception, forcing change. An understanding of the similarities that lie beneath physical differences will alter perception in many areas that affect hiring and marketing.

Ethnicity, unlike race, is not a matter of genes. In fact, many of the most intense ethnic conflicts involve groups of similar appearance. Yugoslavia is a recent example of ethnic hatred based on history, myth, and other factors such as national identity and religion. Such conflicts are not dissimilar to the loyalties and rivalries of opposing high school sports teams or urban gangs. They just have a longer history. Past wins or losses become the stuff of myths; emotionally, it is as if an event passed down from a thousand years ago happened yesterday. Sigmund Freud said these conflicts stemmed from the "narcissism of minor differences."

Everyday contact on more or less equal footing can make a difference. But neither race nor ethnicity myths fall easily. The majority consistently underestimates the depth of pain and anger endured by minorities and the enormous price—emotional and economic—paid by everyone. Minority students segregate themselves in university dining and residence halls to escape the pressure they feel to conform to white myths. A *New York Times* article captured the common feeling in this quote from a freshman living in a black student dorm at Cornell: "I know here no one's going to be asking me why I wear my hair this way." A Chickasaw male, describing how often he felt he had to explain himself to white people, said: "By the end of the day, at a school like this, you're tired."[8]

Even in multicultural America, there remains a deep divide between black and white. Sanford Cloud, Jr., president of the National Conference of Christians and Jews, declared: "It's as though white America is sleepwalking on the edge of a volcano of ethnic and racial differences." The O. J. Simpson verdict let us peer into the heart of that volcano. Several books by African Americans in the 1990s express deep resentment that discrimination persists. Brent Staples, in *Parallel Time: Growing Up in Black and White,* writes of the petty cruelties of whites and "the contained fury that grips even the most outwardly docile black man." *Makes Me Wanna Holler* by Nathan McCall chronicles the self-hatred of a young black male who rejects the society that has rejected him. *Rage of a Privileged Class* by Ellis Cose records the depth of anger of middle-class African-Americans who have "made it" into mainstream America only to remain shut out of the actual power structure.

There is extraordinary danger when any group creates too many peripheral males who have nothing to lose. Humans are mammals, and as uncomfortable as we may be with mammalian behavioral analogies, they do reveal our nature. When too many males become extras in a troop or herd, battles between the dominant males and the aspiring males become increasingly unpredictable and destructive. The peripheral males have nothing to lose, so some will take high risks to get access to power and females, a few will kill themselves and females or create their own group. Similarly, the turmoil in black-white relations in America is a signal that a disproportion of power and privilege exists. How that disproportion is eventually resolved will determine our integrity as a nation and a society, and our ability to move forward into a multiracial future.

SEX, GENDER, AND IMAGE

It is hard to recognize qualities and skills where you once thought few existed. Oregon Steel is an innovative specialty steel mill. When I was working with them on sex-role issues, a supervisor told me that even the best women couldn't fill some of his job openings because the work was too difficult.

I asked him to describe one of these jobs. "Crane operator," he replied. "You need both hands on the controls. One foot operates the foot boom [up or down] or telescope foot [in and out]. The other foot operates the swing brake, regular brake, or the throttle. You have to be able to do everything at once." I said, "That's a woman on the telephone, cooking dinner, and taking care of two kids." He laughed at the image switch and told me some weeks later that he was trying out a woman for one of the positions.

The division of labor between men and women is a gender issue familiar to all of us. But there are many others, all capable of stirring up intense emotions and myths. In some countries, gender can result in immediate death for females unfortunate enough to be born into a traditional family that prefers males—or, for males, life as a bully regardless of personal preference. Gender involves sex, and the sex act traditionally has been viewed by most cultures as one of male dominance and female submission. The growing worldwide battle over female genital mutilation (the descriptive term is clitoridectomy) is an example of the irrationality of these gender myths connected to power.

Gender myth has always cast men as protectors,

warriors, and providers. Now there are marriages in which wives are taking great satisfaction in being the breadwinners—and the husbands are grateful. It was never either/or, but the tendency is to choose sides. As Betty Friedan commented, "Men weren't really the enemy—they were fellow victims suffering from an automated masculine mystique that made them feel unnecessarily inadequate when there were no bears to kill."

The provider element of sex roles was taught to me by my father. He came from a family many generations of which had worked in the coal mines of Wales. He went into the mines at sixteen. A man who worked in dangerous, dirty conditions under the earth was judged a "real man" by his community, not a "toff" (white-collar). He was accorded respect by wife and family. "Why would a man be willing to go down into a mine if it was work a woman could do?" my father said. He would lose the special feelings of courage, satisfaction, and bonding with other men that made the work tolerable.

Men who work as linemen stringing high wires or as combat pilots tell me the same thing. Why would a man take a dangerous or difficult job if it didn't say anything about his masculinity? Some women who take such jobs find themselves sabotaged by male coworkers unwilling to give up their hard-earned status. City Light in Seattle and other power companies have recorded training and safety violations that amounted to thinly disguised assaults on females in nontraditional jobs.

Gender involves family, concepts such as love, responsibility, control, and protection. Changing the work rules, changing the economic balance, and changing the division of labor changes everything at the deepest levels of society. The fear of these changes and the fear of women as equals seem to be worldwide, despite the successes of Margaret Thatcher and Benazir Bhutto. The fear of female equality among some Americans, in our democratic and free society, is explainable perhaps by the narrowness of our Puritan sexual heritage, the violence of much of our male bonding, and the control women have exerted over children.

Gender issues also include sexual orientation. The armed forces in a number of countries openly accept gays. The U.S. military is still grappling with the choices. Do you prefer women in combat aircraft who might have PMS or a person in the barracks next to you who might be a homosexual? How do you maintain the military myths if you let the symbols slide?

The treatment of gays in the military went from "You don't exist" to "We can't see you" to "We don't want you, we'll harass and punish you" to "We'll put up with you." Then came the absurd policy of "Don't ask, don't tell"—a classic solution to image-myth clashes. A change takes place but is not acknowledged. Next year a new ruling will allow "them" to talk about "it" on weekends.

African-American men in the South knew about this strategy years ago. They were allowed to exist in public as long as they were careful not to draw attention to their presence, in particular their sexuality, strength, or masculinity. They could not exhibit power or success openly, but as "boys" they were an accepted part of Southern communities.

DIVERSITY AS A PROCESS

Americans have always taken pride in their diversity, yet we seem to act in ways that deny it. Think about what is required to achieve diversity: the changing of belief systems about intelligence and the relative value of one's own gender, race, or ethnicity. It is an enormous shift that can be very threatening. We naturally want to maintain our personal and cultural images and illusions. We want to hire and work with people who will leave our basic belief system intact. We are often not even conscious that we are excluding anyone and not aware of why we are doing so. Sometimes it is to protect privilege. In other instances, it is a matter of personal comfort or a preference for the familiar. When I was at the University of Washington in Seattle, professors being considered for tenure had to pass the "lunch test": Would you want to eat lunch with this person for twenty years?

Achieving diversity is an especially slow process, like erosion. Schoolbooks, dolls, advertisements, and movies begin to include images of the irregulars. Timberland advertises its boots with a "Give Racism the Boot" slogan, unconcerned that it might hurt sales. Caucasians tell pollsters they are ready to vote for Colin Powell. The irregulars, over time, become regular. The old beliefs become harder to sustain.

Most of us are learning to suspend reactions that are based on myth, emotion, or traditional stereotype and instead become conscious, critical thinkers. New information and experience are replacing old instincts and patterns, moving our responses to others out of our guts and into our minds. There is an increasing acceptance of diversity. The process seems to happen in eight predictable stages:

Stage one. Control based on simply being dominant. The minority member is treated as a savage or servant who is lucky to be associated with the dominant class and therefore benefit from its largesse. Things are as they should be, God is pleased, and it is the natural order. Systems that operate on this model include colonialism, slavery, Nazism, Ku Klux Klan separatism, and apartheid. These are systems that exterminate indigenous peoples, torture enemies, mutilate genitals, allow female infanticide and battering, and institutionalize unequal systems of justice. Those in power are satisfied with the way things are until the economic cost is too high.

Economic energy increases through connection and decreases through forced separation and control. Arbitrary race, gender, and ethnic distinctions endanger the economies and societies of many nations (South Africa, India, the Islamic states, Mexico, Argentina). When too much of the national energy is put into maintaining and enforcing separations, significant increases in quality of life are impossible. Eventually the system of control is challenged.

The process of challenge in America, in this century, has created a consistent expanding of civil rights.

1900	Domestics, miners, Chinese railroad workers
1910	Immigrant laborers, farmers
1920	Women and suffrage
1930	Working men, unions
1940	Displaced persons, citizenship for Native Americans
1950	African Americans, refugees
1960	Women and equality, civil rights, voting rights, Medicare
1970	Seniors, battered women and children
1980	Americans with disabilities, animal rights
1990	Homosexuals, all other minorities

Stage two. Hate based on the belief of the dominant group that anyone different is out to take its women, children, jobs, or possessions. Xenophobia, the fear of strangers or foreigners, is a variant of this. Consultants and authors Bailey Jackson and Evangelina Holvino call organizations in this stage exclusionary; no member of the unacceptable group gets promoted.[9] The Marine Corps is an example (until very recently, the rate at which it promoted minorities was appalling), as are the upper management levels of many corporations and institutions. Denial is common. People say to themselves, "Well, there is really no bias. To help them or hire them would just be reverse discrimination. There are just no qualified candidates with experience."

Stage three. Toleration based on social, legal, moral, or market pressures. Special programs are created, buildings are made wheelchair accessible, formal or informal quotas are set up, and obvious inequalities are dealt with. But the organization is still thinking, "They just aren't as good or as smart as we are." At this stage you hear statements such as "We invited one but he didn't want to join" or "I don't know why they don't live in our neighborhood." Workers forced to accept minority colleagues show their resentment. During the 1994 forest fire season, some female firefighters woke up in the morning to find "Cunt" had been painted on their helmets while they slept.

Stage four. Imitation as a way to pretend all is well. The lunchroom starts serving Mexican food and there is a celebration for Cinco de Mayo. Advertising for the company's products now includes an assortment of "ethnics," depending on the target audience. Able-bodied workers ride around in wheelchairs or wear blindfolds during sensitivity training. More women and minorities are allowed into the organization but not in a way that actually disturbs or threatens the traditional structure or goals. Jackson and Holvino characterize this as a compliance organization.[10] There is an artificial sense of equality that leaves many people tense and wary. Everyone talks acceptance but somehow discrimination is still present. There is often suspicion that the minorities have an unfair advantage: "You know, the only reason he didn't get his promotion was because they put less qualified minorities ahead of him."

Stage five. Redefinition that results in genuine change. Multicultural sensitivity expands and fewer "slips" are made because the new mosaic begins to seem natural. More managers become aware of past discrimination and act to change the pattern. Promotions are announced for more women and minorities; they are, however, seen as deserved. Managers participate in sensitivity training, become more aware of the history and accomplishments of minorities. Color and accent don't command the attention that they used to. Your organization may be here now. The U.S. Army is.

Sometimes this stage produces a fear response among the majority just as it is crossing the bridge to the acceptance of diversity. The fear is the powerful realiza-

---

REVERSE DISCRIMINATION

This exercise will help "regulars" who feel victimized by reverse discrimination to put the situation in perspective. If you are a member of the majority, ask yourself, and then a minority friend, the following questions. Then compare your answers.

Did you ever feel shut out of activities as a child because of your appearance?

Have you ever been denied entrance into a school, hotel, theater, restaurant, swimming pool, toilet, barbershop, meeting, store, or club because of your ethnicity?

Do you think you've ever been turned away from an apartment or rental house, an employment opportunity, training, or a promotion because of your ethnicity?

Have you ever been granted access or advantage because of your gender, appearance, ethnicity, special skills (athletic or music scholarships), parents' position or membership, residence, or kinship?

Have you ever felt people were staring at you, disliking you, making negative comments to you, refusing friendship or contact with you because of your ethnicity?

Has anyone ever said to you, "I didn't want you here, but now that I know you, it's okay"?

Has anyone ever referred to you as "you people," indicating your membership in a "special" group?

---

tion that their legitimate competition has significantly increased. The privilege and advantage of being a member of the majority is gone. Some come to believe that being a female or minority is now an advantage and complaints of reverse discrimination are also heard. The best managers are prepared for this, and they institute new tests and evaluation procedures to preserve fairness in hiring and promotion.

Stage six. *Acceptance* of humanity in all its diversity. The majority looks beyond features and behaviors that used to dictate attitudes and reactions, and instead judges the minority on ability and performance. The organization's leaders begin to have confidence in "different" employees because they are making genuine contributions. This is a deep and permanent human gain, a significant increase in consciousness.

Stage seven. *Forgetting* what all the trouble was about because the differences continue to fade in importance. Managers are comfortable with the competence and contributions of all sorts of people. Teams are more productive and a sense of fairness seems to have developed. Spirits are high and feelings are positive. Managers are able to promote members of the majority without attracting attention from people who used to be part of the minority. This is now a truly multicultural organization.

Stage eight. *Noticing* or encountering a new group of irregulars. They don't seem to be related to any of the other "different" people that the new majority has come to accept. So the process starts all over again, possibly with this refrain from the modified majority: "We are already happy living with, working with, and dating African Americans, Italians, Catholics, and Hungarians. Do we have to talk to Muslims and homosexuals too?"

THE NEXT MINORITY

Maybe the next minority will show up on television talk shows. I remember one program that began with a male,

middle-aged transvestite on stage alone. He wore an un-
attractive dress and the audience was clearly not sympathetic. Then his wife of twenty-six years joined him. She
said he was a good, loving husband who understood
women. He only wore dresses in the backyard on weekends. The audience said, "That's okay for you, but . . ."

Then his three adult children appeared. He had been
a great dad, coached Little League. They had even devised a signal to warn him when an outsider was ap-
proaching the backyard. The audience said, "Yes, but we
don't want to work with a weirdo. . . ."

Then his boss came onstage. The man had worked
for the same company for twenty years and was a good
employee. The company had found out about the dresses
seven years into his employment, but let it go. After all,
he only wore the dresses in the backyard. . . .

By now the audience was weighing the positives
and negatives of the man's behavior. The questions began to shift and the reactions seemed more sympathetic.
The last question was a comment: "You know, you
would look better in red." The audience had decided that
his real problem was that he had no taste.

When I wonder who will be next, I am reminded of
an episode that a friend experienced. She goes to soccer
games with her ten-year-old and sits with other parents.
At a recent game, two mothers in front of her were argu-
ing. They were a lesbian couple, and their sons were half
brothers, four months apart in age. The boys have the
same sperm-donor father, who was also at the game. The
argument was about his new wife, who is developmen-
tally disabled. The mothers believed that it was wrong
for him to have married a woman of "limited" intelligence. My friend has since been seen wandering around
with her mouth hanging open, trying to form the word
"What?" So when people ask me when this process of
new minorities arriving in our midst will come to an end,
I reply, "Never!" After all, we still have extraterrestrials
to meet.

There is no choice but to accept humanity in all its

forms. In the years ahead, the continual mixing of genetic pools from one generation to the next will gradually blur the physical characteristics of race and ethnicity. As women and men blend their roles and skills, we will all be wiser. Character and competence will be the most useful measures of a person's value.

Expect, in the meantime, to encounter new minorities. Diversity training—seminars and discussion groups led by experts in the field—help get organizations through the process of acceptance. It's useful to first check out the experiences of other companies or organizations. A young industry, like computers, faces less resistance when undertaking diversity training than, for example, the defense industry or firefighters. As a leader, evaluate the levels of resistance that minorities face and the beliefs behind it. How can you help change those beliefs? Encourage your people to speak openly about their feelings. Look for ways to bring diverse groups together on some common ground so they will get to know each other as individuals.

Learn *from* other racial and ethnic groups, not just *about* them. Join an organization where you are a minority. Get involved with student exchange programs, American Friends Service Committee, Rotary International, or American Field Service. Volunteer to coach or tutor the children of any group significantly different from your own. Get your children involved. They need the experience, too.

Above all, practice "zero tolerance" for racism or sexism. The United States Army started doing this with its cadets at West Point and its regular units in the 1970s. The army has done a good job, but it has the advantage of being able to enforce such policies—with the stockade. We have to rely on our own courage.

The best place to look for insight into managing diversity is inside yourself. What gains or losses do you believe you will face if equality becomes acceptable in your workplace, your neighborhood, or the world? Ask yourself if the gains outnumber the losses. In your role as manager, be alert for individuals who feel they are losing power or think their traditions are endangered. They will work hard to sabotage the advancement of a group that seems threatening. Shared power and status always strengthen an organization. The acceptance of diversity and the ability to profit from the unique intelligence and skills of individuals, no matter how diverse, are key skills for the future success of any organization. Leaders and managers should be prepared to intervene and handle the anxiety, anger, and tension that are part of such deep and personal change. In a customer-driven, global marketplace, multicultural intelligence will be a core factor in a company's future success.

Epilogue

" . . . the world offers itself to your imagination,
calls to you like the wild geese, harsh and exciting—
over and over announcing your place
in the family of things."

—MARY OLIVER, "WILD GEESE"

THIS BOOK HAS BEEN about the thinking skills that create visionaries: perspective, pattern recognition, cultural knowledge, flexibility, vision, energy, intelligence, and global values. Leadership in the twenty-first century will also require a heightened awareness of what the poet Mary Oliver calls "the family of things," a context for what otherwise is an overwhelming kaleidoscope of change. With these thinking skills, you will have a framework for the pieces of the complex puzzle of change, and you can begin to form a picture. You can begin to know where you fit.

The developing image of the future, for the leader or the individual who has the thinking skills to perceive it, is an exciting one. It is not a future with man as a robotic cyborg but with man possessed of a heightened intelligence. The greatest future challenge for both leaders and individuals is not whether they will be able to "surf the net" but whether they can effectively lead and participate in a knowledge-based workforce. We are all becoming more individual and, at the same time, more a part of a larger whole, whether as an executive of a multinational corporation, a manager, a worker, an entrepreneur, or a citizen. As increasing self-knowledge expands our individuality, the shrinking globe and marketplace will pull us together and increase our interdependence. Leadership will require a deeper and wider consciousness, perception, vision, and wisdom. The skills to think in the future tense will be imperative.

Most of us do think about the future. Americans have always been pioneers, used to loading up our wagons and heading for a new frontier. The benefits on this new frontier for open-minded leaders and workers will be many. You will be more secure and in control of the quality and purpose of your work. You will find it easier to inspire a diverse group of colleagues. You will make better decisions. There will be more companies and organizations that will respect your abilities, your individuality, and your values. You will have the freedom to work at the highest levels of your capability. You will become more comfortable as you become more able to adapt to change. You will run a more ethics-based business. You will operate in an egalitarian organization. You will live in a safer world. Global mobility will release us from many of the distortions and absurdities of worn-out myths and historical allegiances. We cannot demonize enemies or demean workers if geography, business, and organizational structures no longer separate us.

The intelligence for leadership will require a new awareness of ourselves and others as we consciously evolve, utilizing skills of a higher and higher level. The direction in which we have been traveling for millions of years is not a new order but an expanding order; we are becoming an increasingly aware civilization in increasingly intimate communication. Technological change is creating greater access to information; economic change is creating shared global economies; demographic change is generating greater diversity and new business and social contacts. Cultures are intermingling. We ourselves are being transformed.

A global marketplace and workforce are creating stronger alliances; a world brain pool is becoming a world gene pool. A global client will generate respect for diversity and interdependent prosperity. A worldwide information net will equalize access to education and wealth. A young man in Zaire or Siberia will not have to migrate; he can write software for Netscape in his own village. Satellites and telecommuters will create an environment for greater equality, stable economies, and a less fragmented world. Worldwide literacy, a shared market, and an international language will all have a significant impact on the extent of our knowledge of and our behavior toward each other.

When more people know more, when communication is instantaneous, tyranny and the creation of political illusions will become more difficult. When computers quickly collate data, documents, and policies, it is harder to create disinformation or to manipulate images. Corporations will benefit, not just from the same communication pluses as governments, but also from deregulation and reduced litigation. Mediation and arbitration will be the conflict resolution models of the future. The expansion of access to accurate information and the elimination of traditional constrictions and illusions will allow all of us to stop pretending much earlier in our lives. There will be a new freedom to grow up and take responsibility for what we know and do.

It is easier to lead complex organizations with informed, empowered, accountable colleagues. But it is still exhausting. As *New York Times* columnist Anna Quindlen put it, "We are awash in the revealed world." There is pain here, the grief process that accompanies most change. But if you think in the future tense, you will become aware of the gap between what you believe you know and the beliefs of some of those you must lead. It is this gap that, in times of such change, can drive you crazy. The skills to think in the future tense and the recognition that change is often predictable will reduce your anxiety. These skills will provide an awareness of awareness, the knowledge that there are many perceptions of and possible responses to the same events. Your "new mind" will force you more and more frequently to ask what your business is about, what leadership means, who you are, and whether or not you are heading in the right direction.

The expanding concept of what it means to be a leader will be revolutionary in all areas of human exchange. It will go way beyond mastering new technology and succeeding in a new economy. Leadership will require new contracts, new civility, and ultimately a new intimacy between diverse groups.

Contracts, whether business or social, set up principles of behavior, action, and reciprocity. They are a practical recognition of enforceable interdependence. With change, many of our agreements will have to be renegotiated. Inevitably, when existing agreements are renegotiated, values are questioned and there is a loss of what was once thought to be right. When chaos and ambivalent leadership prevent the renegotiation of agreements, we are left in between the old and the new. The in-between feels like failure, that nothing is right or sacred and there is a moral void. Few sense this as a historical step up in civilization; many people feel betrayed. Still others try to reintroduce the old agreements. When the chaos of renegotiation is resolved and a new set of agreements is accepted, stability returns.

Leadership becomes most difficult when it requires a step up in civility, the acceptance of diversity, and new values. Despite the current tribal and ethnic battles, international leaders are increasingly nonviolent. The paradox of a lack of muscle in our work and the seemingly endless violence in our entertainment is also a clue that aggression is becoming a cultural death rattle. But each new limit on violence produces disorientation for some as it redefines leadership for others.

The headhunters of the Philippines, the Ilongot hill tribes, provide a telling illustration.[1] They believed it was necessary to "take a head" to become a man. When headhunting was outlawed in 1972, their worldview was shattered. Many of the Ilongot men slipped into depression, lamenting their loss of place, freedom and battle. It is ironic that "headhunter" now refers to high-level employment recruiters.

What will replace the myths, rituals, symbols, leaders, and lodges of our past? René Girard, in his spellbinding book, *Things Hidden Since the Foundation of the World,* wonders if we can accept the "nothingness" that we will face while we fill our souls with new wisdom.[2] Many of the ancient questions of life now require new answers. But if the quality of a civilization is defined by the intimacy and extent of its communication, the maintaining of its agreements, and the expansion of its commitment to nonviolence, then we are on the right track. We will continue to develop our capacity to reinforce, expand, and clarify what is most important to our work and to our lives.

The pieces of the puzzle may still seem chaotic, the images are not all recognizable, but we do have the will and the skills to see the future. Although our circumstances are profoundly ambivalent, our minds are open as they have never been before. As we stand beside Jacob Shamier's grave to "tell him the news," we each have an assignment: to perceive the problems that we face and achieve insight into the beliefs that have produced them. We must be willing to participate, to intervene—and be able to handle the anxiety, resistance, and anger that come with intervention. Be alert to the siren song of nostalgia; be patient with the missteps of transition; tread lightly; imagine other possibilities; look around; think ahead.

When more of the pieces of the puzzle of change fit

into place and we can actually see the future because we are in it, we will have the security of knowing where we, too, fit. We will pay a price for the current technological, economic, and cultural changes because of their magnitude, but we will also reap rich rewards when new contracts are finally in place. We will find new excitement in our work as well as in our relationships. We will follow our leaders with more confidence and become better leaders ourselves. We will lead by growing closer to each other. We will move forward by going deeper.

Notes

Introduction

1. I first heard this phrase from Dr. Edward Lindaman, visionary president of Whitworth College (Spokane, Washington) from 1970 to 1980.
2. Durkheim, Emile, *Suicide: A Sociological Study* (Springfield, Ill.: The Free Press, 1951; first published in 1897).
3. Marshall McLuhan was a Canadian specialist in culture and technology at McGill University in Toronto. He was an English professor, a maverick who conducted seminars in media communications. His books, *The Mechanical Bride: Folklore of Industrial Man* (1951), *The Gutenberg Galaxy* (1962), *Understanding Media* (1964), *The Medium Is the Message* (1967), *War and Peace in the Global Village* (1968), and *Culture Is Our Business* (1970), made him an icon and a myth.

Skill 1

1. McLuhan, Marshall, *Understanding Media: The Extensions of Man* (New York: The New American Library, 1964).
2. Kopp, Sheldon, *This Side of Tragedy* (Palo Alto, Calif.: Science and Behavior, 1977).
3. Senge, Peter, *The Fifth Discipline* (New York: Doubleday Currency, 1990).
4. Ibid.
5. Gleick, James, *Chaos: Making a New Science* (New York: Penguin Books, 1987).

Skill 2

1. Rotstein, Ronald, *The Future* (New York: Carol Publishing Group, 1990).

2. U.S. Department of Commerce, *1995 Statistical Abstract of the United States.*

Skill 4

1. Ferguson, Marilyn, *The Aquarian Conspiracy* (Los Angeles, Calif.: J. P. Tarcher, Inc., 1980).

Skill 5

1. Morrow, Lance, "The Bad Old Days," *Time,* May 8, 1995.
2. Coontz, Stephanie, *The Way We Never Were* (New York: Basic Books, 1992).
3. Management Case Study, prepared by US West, undated.

Skill 6

1. Beck, Nuala, *Shifting Gears: Thriving in the New Economy* (Toronto: Harper Perennial, 1993) and *Excelerate: Growing in the New Economy* (Toronto: HarperCollins, 1995).
2. "Brain Gyms," *Newsweek,* November 8, 1993.
3. "Low Pay and Closed Doors," *New York Times,* March 10, 1994.
4. Socratic Dialogue, Charles Ogletree, Professor of Law, Harvard University, Cambridge, Mass.
5. Oster, Patrick, "The Fast Track Leads Overseas," *BusinessWeek,* November 1, 1993.

Skill 7

1. FairTest, Cambridge, Mass.
2. "California Learning Assessment System," *New York Times,* May 4, 1994.
3. Gardner, Howard, *Frames of Mind* (New York: Basic Books, 1985).
4. Browning, Geil, *The Perfect Creative and Productive Team* (Englewood, Colo.: The Browning Group, 1996).
5. De Bono, Edward, *De Bono's Thinking Course* (New York: Facts on File, 1982).
6. De Bono, Edward, *Six Thinking Hats* (London: Penguin Books, 1985).
7. Morrison, Ian, *Future Tense* (New York: Morrow, 1994).

Skill 8

1. Stratford, Sherman, "Wanted: Company Change Agents," *Fortune,* December 11, 1995.
2. Stetson-Rodriguez, Marian, *New York Times* interview, April 18, 1994.

3. Hudson Institute, *Workforce 2000* (Indianapolis, Ind., 1987).
4. "How to Make Diversity Pay," *Fortune*, August 8, 1994.
5. Medical school admissions records, University of Washington.
6. Bowen, Asta, "The American Experiment," *Post-Intelligencer*, Seattle, Wash., December 26, 1993.
7. Menozzi, Paola, and Piazza, Alberta, *The History and Geography of Human Genes* (Princeton, N.J.: Princeton University Press, 1995).
8. Winerip, Michael, "In School," *New York Times*, April 20, 1994.
9. Jackson, Bailey, and Holvino, Evangelina, "Developing Multicultural Organizations," *Journal of Religion and the Applied Behavioral Sciences*, Fall 1988.
10. Ibid.

Epilogue

1. Rosaldo, Michelle Z., *Knowledge and Passion: Ilongot Notions of Self and Social Life* (New York: Cambridge University Press, 1980).
2. Girard, René, *Things Hidden Since the Foundation of the World* (Stanford, Calif.: Stanford University Press, 1987).

Bibliography

Abrams, Malcolm. *More Future Stuff.* New York: Penguin Books, 1991.

Abrams, Malcolm, and Bernstein, Harriet. *Future Stuff.* New York: Penguin Books, 1989.

Allman, William F. *The Stone Age Present.* New York: Simon & Schuster, 1994.

Bardkow, Jerome; Cosmides, Leda; and Tooby, John. *The Adapted Mind.* New York: Oxford University Press, 1992.

Barker, Joel Arthur. *Paradigms: The Business of Discovering the Future.* New York: HarperBusiness, 1992.

Bateson, Gregory. *Steps to an Ecology of Mind.* New York: Ballantine, 1972.

Beck, Nuala. *Shifting Gears: Thriving in the New Economy.* Toronto: HarperPerennial, 1993.

———. *Excelerate: Growing in the New Economy.* Toronto: HarperCollins, 1995.

Bly, Robert. *Iron John.* Reading, Mass.: Addison-Wesley Publishing Company, 1990.

Bruner, Jerome. *Actual Minds, Possible Worlds.* Cambridge, Mass.: Harvard University Press, 1986.

Buechner, Thomas A. *Norman Rockwell: A 60-Year Perspective.* New York: Harry N. Abrams, 1972.

Campbell, Joseph. *The Hero with a Thousand Faces.* Princeton, N.J.: Princeton University Press, 1972.

———. *Myths to Live By.* New York: Bantam Books, 1972.

———. *The Power of Myth.* New York: Doubleday, 1988.

Capra, Fritjof. *The Turning Point.* New York: Simon & Schuster, 1982.

Chafetz, Michael D. *Smart for Life.* New York: Penguin Books, 1992.

Coontz, Stephanie. *The Way We Never Were.* New York: Basic Books, 1992.

Cousins, Norman. *Anatomy of an Illness.* New York: Norton Books, 1979.

Danforth, John C. *Resurrection: The Confirmation of Clarence Thomas.* New York: Viking, 1994.

Darwin, Charles. *The Origin of Species.* New York: Penguin Books, 1968.

Davis, Stan, and Davidson, Bill. *2020 Vision.* New York: Simon & Schuster, 1991.

De Bono, Edward. *De Bono's Thinking Course.* New York: Facts on File, 1982.

———. *Opportunities.* London: Penguin Books, 1978.

———. *Practical Thinking.* London: Penguin Books, 1971.

———. *Six Thinking Hats.* London: Penguin Books, 1985.

———. *Teaching Thinking.* London: Penguin Books, 1976.

Drucker, Peter F. *Managing for the Future.* New York: Truman Talley Books/Dutton, 1992.

Durkheim, Emile. *Suicide: A Sociological Study.* Springfield, Ill.: Free Press, 1951 (first published in 1897).

Eisler, Benita. *Private Lives: Men and Women of the Fifties.* New York: Franklin Watts, 1986.

Eisler, Riane. *The Chalice and the Blade.* San Francisco: HarperSanFrancisco, 1987.

Etzioni, Amitai. *The Spirit of Community.* New York: Crown Publishers, 1993.

Evans, Christopher. *The Micro Millennium.* New York: Washington Square Press, 1979.

Fanning, John, and Maniscalco, Rosemary. *Workstyles to Fit Your Lifestyle: Everyone's Guide to Temporary Employment.* Englewood Cliffs, N.J.: Prentice-Hall, 1994.

Ferguson, Marilyn. *The Aquarian Conspiracy.* Los Angeles: J. P. Tarcher, 1980.

Fox, Matthew. *The Reinvention of Work.* New York: HarperCollins, 1994.

Gardner, Howard. *Creating Minds.* New York: Basic Books, 1993.

———. *Frames of Mind.* New York: Basic Books, 1985.

———. *Multiple Intelligences: The Theory in Practice.* New York: Basic Books, 1993.

———. *To Open Minds.* New York: Basic Books, 1989.

Gleick, James. *Chaos.* New York: Penguin Books, 1987.

Halacy, D. S., Jr. *Cyborg: Evolution of the Superman.* New York: Harper & Row, 1965.

Hammer, Michael, and Champy, James. *Reengineering the Corporation: A Manifesto for Business Revolution.* New York: HarperBusiness, 1993.

Handy, Charles. *The Age of Unreason.* Boston: Harvard Business School Press, 1989.

Hirsch, E. D., Jr. *Cultural Literacy.* Boston: Houghton Mifflin, 1987.

Howard, Michael C., and Dunaif-Hattis, Janet. *Anthropology: Understanding Human Adaptation.* New York: HarperCollins, 1992.

Jung, Carl G. *Collected Works of Carl Gustav Jung.* 20 vols. Translated by R. F. C. Hull. Edited by H. Read, M. Fordham, G. Adler, and W. McGuire. Bollingen Series XX. Princeton, N.J.: Princeton University Press, 1953–79.

———. *Memories, Dreams, Reflections.* Rev. ed. Recorded and edited by A. Jaffe. Translated by R. Winston and C. Winston. New York: Pantheon, 1973.

Kennedy, Paul. *Preparing for the Twenty-first Century.* New York: Random House, 1993.

Kuhn, Thomas S. *The Structure of Scientific Revolutions.* 2nd ed. Chicago: The University of Chicago Press, 1962.

Laing, R. D. *The Politics of Experience.* New York: Pantheon, 1978.

Lasch, Christopher. *The Revolt of the Elites and the Betrayal of Democracy.* New York: W. W. Norton, 1995.

Lazear, David. *Seven Ways of Knowing.* 2nd ed. Palatine, Ill.: Skylight Publishing, 1991.

Madhubuti, Haki. *Black Men: Obsolete, Single, Dangerous? The African American Family in Transition.* Chicago: Third World Press, 1990.

Maynard, Jr., Herman Bryant. *The Fourth Wave.* San Francisco: Berrett-Koehler Publishers, 1993.

McLuhan, Marshall. *Understanding Media: The Extensions of Man.* New York: The New American Library, 1964.

McLuhan, Marshall, and Fiore, Quentin. *The Medium Is the Message.* New York: Simon & Schuster, 1989.

Menozzi, Paola, and Piazza, Alberta. *The History and Geography of Human Genes.* Princeton, N.J.: Princeton University Press, 1995.

Morrison, Ian. *Future Tense.* New York: Morrow, 1994.

Naisbitt, John. *Global Paradox.* New York: William Morrow, 1994.

Naisbitt, John, and Aburdene, Patricia. *Megatrends 2000.* New York: William Morrow, 1990.

Nalle Schafer, Edith. *Our Remarkable Memory.* Washington, D.C.: Starhill Press, 1988.

Nanus, Burt. *Visionary Leadership.* San Francisco: Jossey-Bass, 1992.

Oliver, Mary. "Wild Geese." In *New and Selected Poems.* Boston: Beacon Press, 1992.

Ornstein, Robert. *Evolution of Consciousness.* Englewood Cliffs, N.J.: Prentice-Hall, 1991.

Peters, Tom. *Liberation Management.* New York: Fawcett Columbine, 1992.

Pritchett, Price, and Pound, Ron. *High-Velocity Culture Change.* Dallas, Tex.: Pritchett Publishing Company, 1993.

Research Alert. *Future Vision.* Naperville, Ill.: Sourcebooks Trade, 1991.

Rheingold, Howard. *The Virtual Community: Homesteading on the Electronic Frontier.* Reading, Mass.: Addison-Wesley, 1993.

Rorvik, David. *As Man Becomes Machine.* Garden City, N.Y.: Doubleday, 1971.

Rosaldo, Michelle Z. *Knowledge and Passion: Ilongot Notions of Self and Social Life.* New York: Cambridge University Press, 1980.

Ross-Macdonald, Malcolm, and Hassell, Michael. *Life in the Future.* New York: Doubleday, 1977.

Rotstein, Ronald D. *The Future.* New York: Carol Publishing Group, 1990.

Senge, Peter M. *The Fifth Discipline.* New York: Doubleday Currency, 1990.

Shekerjian, Denise. *Uncommon Genius.* New York: Penguin Books, 1990.

Stacey, Ralph D. *Managing the Unknowable.* San Francisco: Jossey-Bass, 1992.

Tarnas, Richard. *The Passion of the Western Mind.* New York: Ballantine Books, 1993.

Taylor, Stu. *How to Turn Trends into Fortunes Without Getting Left in the Dust.* New York: Carol Publishing Group, 1993.

Teilhard de Chardin, Pierre. *The Future of Man.* New York: HarperCollins, 1964 (originally published in 1959).

Templeton, John Marks. *Looking Forward: The Next Forty Years.* New York: HarperBusiness, 1993.

Thurow, Lester. *Head to Head.* New York: Warner Books, 1992.

Tichy, Noel M. *The Transformational Leader.* New York: John Wiley, 1986.

Walden, Gene, and Lawler, Edmund O. *Marketing Masters.* New York: HarperBusiness, 1993.

Weber, Max. *The Protestant Ethic and the Spirit of Capitalism.* New York: Charles Scribner's Sons, 1958.

Wheatley, Margaret J. *Leadership and the New Science.* San Francisco: Berrett-Koehler Publications, 1994.

Wittgenstein, Ludwig. *Philosophical Investigations.* Translated by G. E. M. Anscombe. New York: Macmillan, 1968.

Wright, Robert. *The Moral Animal.* New York: Pantheon Books, 1994.

Acknowledgments

A THANK-YOU to my editors for their intelligence and skill, Noel Greenwood, Fred Hills, Burton Beals, and Janine Dallas Steffan. Thank you for a supreme effort to my administrative assistants and computer whizzes Jo Harris and Sarah Herres Powers. A thank-you for her wit and intelligence to my researcher and good friend Elizabeth Miller.

Thank you to the following people for their support and willingness to laugh whenever we needed it; the number-one survival skill is a sense of humor: Bruce and Sue Berglund, Charlotte Bottoms, Linda Jo Bowyer, Adina Cherry, Rafferty and Woofie Evans, Devon James, Marjorie and Ken Johnson, Harry and Linda Macrae, Robin and Kay Norman, Daisye Orr, Michael Herres Powers, Rick Simonson, Andrew and Jenni Snowden, Diana and Deen Stice, Alberta and Homer Stone, the librarians at the Burien Branch of the King County Public Library, the staff at the Seahurst post office, and the couriers of UPS and Federal Express.

Index

absolutes, 196
academics, lodges, 137–138
acceptance
  of diversity, 224
  stage of grief, 150
acculturation, 106
action, 166–167
advertising
  elaboration, 64
  marketing images, 85–86
  in new magazines, 99–100
  signal of change, 97
  use of nostalgia, 129
affirmative action, 212
African Americans
  books by, 216
  "don't draw attention," 219
  in the 1950s, 132
age
  and perspective, 35
  and vegetables, 110
Age of Unreason, The, 173
air travel, and elaboration, 65
alternatives, 191–193
  alternative energy, 159
  finding, 125
  your experiences, 194–195
  team-building exercises, 192
AMA (American Medical Association), 29

ambivalence, 15–16
American Express, 62
American Medical Association.
  See AMA
analytical thinkers, 186
Anatomy of an Illness, 121
Andreotti, Giulio, 85
Angelou, Maya, 153
anger, 149
  and humor, 175
animals
  and class issues, 37
  meat as condiment, 54–55
Annapolis, lodge code, 136
anomalies, 100
"anomie" state, 20
Argyris, Chris, 44
Army, the future, 82–83
  zero tolerance, 226
arts, the, and change, 95–96
Asian Americans, 181
assimilation, 106
AT&T
  cellular phones, 58
  clinging to old myths, 80

baby-boomers, and trends, 56
bachelors, the 1950s, 133
balancing your life, 176–178
  benefits of relaxing, 39

Baldwin, James, 21
bargaining, 149–150
Barker, Joel, 121
barriers to thinking, 196–200
Beauty and the Beast, 92, 93
Beck, Nuala, 157, 159
Beckett, John, 100
Bell Labs, 51
Bennis, Warren, 139
best-seller lists, 98–99
Biden, Joseph, 84
Big, 47
big-game hunting, 55
Bill Cosby Show, The, 87
black-hat thinker, 191
Black Like Me, 47
blue-hat thinker, 191
Bly, Robert, 33–34
body, interest in, 54–55
body/kinesthetic intelligence,
    183
Body Shop, 205
Boeing Aircraft, 149
Boise Cascade, 29
Bold and the Beautiful, The, 87
books
    by African Americans, 216
    best-seller lists, 98–99
    children's, 99
    science fiction, 94–95
Boosler, Elaine, 40
Bowen, Asta, 214
brain
    capacity of, 180
    middle brain, 179–180
    mind gyms, 164
    short-term memory, 30
    we must adapt, 23–24
Branson, Richard, 44
British class system, 36–37
Browning, Geil, 185
burnout, 20
business, 79–83
    "business dance," 147
    and myths, 79–83

Campbell, Joseph, 168
Care of the Soul, 99
Celestine Prophecy, The, 99
census, 214–215
Challenger, 148–149
change
    and age, 35
    dysfunctional, 122–123
    evaluating, 142
    flexibility, 108–111
    predicting, 56–59
    processes of, 106–108
    styles of, 111–123
        coercion, 122–123
        exception, 122
        incremental, 111–120
        pendulum swing, 123
        systemic, 120–122
    surprise changes, 124–126
    symbols and myths, 83–86
    threatening, 104
    transition, 126–127
chaos, 67–68
    tolerance for, 45
Charles, Steve, 59
children
    age and change, 35
    children's books, 99
    children's myths, 92–94
    as cyborgs, 17–18
    humor and intelligence, 175
    new experiences, 27
"civilization syndrome," 55
civil rights, 221
Clark, Harvey, 132
class systems, 36–37
Clinton, Bill, 43, 85
Cloud, Sanford, Jr., 216
CNN, 97–98, 205
coaches, change in tactics,
    161
Coca-Cola, 208, 209
coercion, change by, 122–123
"coincidental adaptation," 69
Cold War, 74

communications
  and cultural change, 107
  skills, 165–166
comparative thinking, 69
computers
  age and fear of, 35
  buying, 113–114
  and children, 16, 17–18
  electronic memories, 30
  the Internet, 60–62
  smart offices, 18
  why they're addictive, 38
  and work habits, 19
conceptual thinkers, 186
conflict resolution, 165–166
conformity, 198–199
confusion, and chaos, 45
contentment, 190
context, and memory, 32
continuing education, 164–165
control, 220–221
  blue-hat thinker, 191
  outside control, 107
Coontz, Stephanie, 132
corporate cultures, 139–143
"corridor principle," 69
Cose, Ellis, 216
Cousins, Norman, 121
creativity, 182
  green-hat thinker, 191
  and humor, 175
C-SPAN, 98
culture, 22–23. *See also* myths
    and symbols
  "cultural blues," 15
  cultural evolution, 106–107
  cultural loss, 106
  "cultural pollution," 87–88
  knowledge of, 42–43
customers do the work, 162–
    163
cutting edge, 163–164
"cyber" age, 17
Cyberpunks, 63
cyborgs, 17

Dallas, 87
"dance of life," reversals, 66
Dances with Wolves, 89
danger, sense of, 155
death rattles, 101–103
De Bono, Edward, 186–187
  hats, 190–191
Demming, W. Edward, 140–141,
    188
demographic changes, 21–22
denial, 148–149
diffusion, 106
Discovery Channel, 97
Disney
  messages and metaphors, 76
  overseas attractions, 87–88
distortions, 33–38
  age, 35
  class, 36–37
  electronic media, 37–38
  gender, 35–36
  self-righteousness, 34–35
diversity, 207–211
  accepting, 219–224
  gender, 217–219
  the next minority, 224–227
  race/ethnicity myths, 214–217
  racial categories, 214–215
  in the workforce, 211–214
Doctor, The, 47
driving forces, 53–55
Drucker, Peter, 137, 175
Dunlap, Albert, J., 82
Durkheim, Emile, 20
dysfunctional change, 122–123
  by coercion, 122–123
  by exception, 122
  pendulum swing, 123

Economist, The, 45
education
  continuing, 164–165
  jobs of the future, 158
  money management, 168–
    169

"ego integrity," 195
Egypt, power of myths, 101
Einstein, Albert, 183, 185
Eisenhower, Dwight D., 132
Eisler, Benita, 132
elaboration, 63–65
electronic media
  as a distortion, 37–38
  expansion, 62–63
Embracing the Light, 56
emotion
  EQ, 195
  hot buttons, 46–47
  and memory, 32
  red-hat thinker, 191
emotional quotient (EQ), 195
empathy, 47–48
energy, 153–154
  creating, 160–170
  multitasking, 162–163
  observing, 160–161
  and security, 153
  at work, 156–160
engineered food, 63
entrepreneurs
  characteristics, 68–70
  resilience, 43–44
environment, in the 1950s, 133
EQ (emotional quotient), 195
Erikson, Erik, 195
ethnicity, 214–217
ethnocentrism, 42–43
eugenic sterilization, 133
evaluations, 168
  incremental change, 117–
    118
Evans, Ted, 209
exception, change by, 122
exercise, example of change,
    112
experience
  and behavior, 27–28
  overseas, 210
  think about, 194–195
exploration, and change, 116

extension, 56–59, 62–63
  the Internet, 60–62
Exxon, symbols, 80–81

FairTest, 181
fairy tales, 92–93
  alternative versions, 99
family
  balance, 170–172
  impact of work on, 169
fast footwork, 69
fear of the future, 28
Feigenbaum, Mitchell, 50
fiber optics, 158
Fifth Discipline, The, 44
financial interests, 168–169
flexibility, 69
  portable skills, 173–174
  testing, 108–109
    language test, 110–111
    vegetable test, 110
flextime, 169
flow analysis, 193
forecasts, 202–204
foreign countries
  trends in, 101
  work hours, 169–170
forgetting, 224
frame of reference, 31–32
France, Euro Disney, 88
Freud, Sigmund, 184
Friedan, Betty, 218
future
  exploring, 201–206
  importance of perspective,
    28
  industries, 158–159
  jobs, 157–158
  new lodges, 152
  recognizing, 50
  skills needed, 24
  understand the past, 128
Future Tense, 201
"fuzzy logic," intuition, 40–
    41

Gandhi, Mohandas, 184
Gardner, Howard, 182, 184
Gauguin, 32
gender
  myths, 217–219
  perspective, 35–36
  thinking processes, 200
General Electric, 208–209
genetics, 159
genital mutilation, 101
geographic adaptability, 174
Gerstner, Lou, 158
Gleick, James, 50, 54
global citizens, 207
global values. *See* diversity
global village, 86–89
Goodman, Nelson, 182
Graham, Martha, 183
green-hat thinker, 191
grief/nostalgia syndrome, 148
  acceptance, 150
  anger, 149
  bargaining, 149–150
  denial, 148
  rebuilding, 150–151
Griffen, John Howard, 47
guns, smart, 62
gut responses, 199–200
  intuition, 40–41

Hayles, V. Robert, 201
Handy, Charles, 53, 173
Hatch, Orrin, 84
hate, 221
hierarchies
  corporate cultures, 139–140
  and lodges, 135
Hill, Anita, 83–84, 197
history
  cultural, 42–43
  and nostalgia, 131
  personal, 41–42
*History and Geography of Human
  Genes, The*, 215
Holvino, Evangelina, 221, 222

homosexuality
  fear of, 35–36
  magazines, 99
  the military, 219
  the 1950s, 132
hot buttons, 46–47
Houston, Whitney, 87
How We Die, 56
Hudson, Rock, 96
humility, 193–194
humor, 40, 175
hypothetical thought, 69

IBM
  the "Intranet," 68
  misperception, 29, 33, 52
  symbol of uniformity, 81
illusion, the 1950s, 131–135
image, 217–219
imagination, and insight, 40–
  41
imitation, 222
immediate gratification, 196–
  197
immigration, 21
Imperial Chemical Industries,
  151
India, gender/class changes, 101
incest, in the 1950s, 132–133
incremental change, 111–120
  examples
    buying a computer, 113–
      114
    career change, 119–120
    exercise, 112
  seven basic steps, 114–118
individual self, 171
industries, the future, 158–159
  alternative energy, 159
  fiber optics, 158
  genetics, 159
  lasers, 159
  nanotechnology, 159
  photonics, 158–159
  space colonization, 159

information
  the Internet, 60–62
  revealing, 167
  styles of processing, 185–187
  use of multiple sources, 44
ingenuity, 69
innovation, 106
In Search of Excellence, 121
insight, 40–41
instinctual responses, 199–200
integration, and change,
      116–117
intelligence, 179–181
  being too smart, 198
  forms of, 182–185
    body/kinesthetic, 183
    interpersonal, 183–184
    intrapersonal, 184
    logical/mathematical,
      182–183
    musical/rhythmic, 183
    practical, 184
    spiritual, 184
    verbal/linguistic, 182
    visual/spatial, 183
  "high diversity IQs," 208
  and humility, 193–194
  IQ tests, 181
  "middle brain," 179–180
  thinking skills, 190–195
  thinking styles, 185–187
interdependence, 21–22
International Television News
      (ITN), 98
Internet, 60–62
interpersonal intelligence,
      183–184
intrapersonal intelligence, 184
intuition, 40–41
invention, 106
IQ tests, 181
  and music, 183
Ishmael, 99
ITN (International Television
      News), 98

Jackson, Bailey, 221, 222
Japanese
  America as model, 88
  and changing myths, 86
  elaboration, 63
  and humility, 194
  in the 1950s, 133–134
  recognizing patterns, 51
  jobs of the future, 157–158
  smart work, 19–21
Johnson, Magic, 96–97
Jordan, Michael, 183
journals, 72
Jung, Carl, 184

Katzenbach, Jon, 208
Kelly, Kevin, 45
Kennedy, Ted, 84
King, Martin Luther, Jr., 184
Kissebah, Ahmed, 55
Kopp, Sheldon, 41
Kraft General Foods, 62

L.A. Law, 87
landing, and change, 117
language
  flexibility test, 110–111
  indicator of change, 70–
      71
  and symbols, 78–79
lasers, 159
lateral thinking, 186–187
lawyers, lodges, 137
leadership
  enlightened, 143–147
  and high school, 90
  influence of myths, 80
  myth and reality, 75–76
Leland, John, 97
lifework self, 171
Lightner, Candy, 70
Lincoln, Abraham, 184
LINK Resources, 162
Lion King, The, 76
Little Mermaid, The, 92

lodges, 135
  cardinal rule, 139
  corporate cultures, 139–143
  examples, 136–138
    academics, 137–138
    lawyers, 137
    physicians, 136–137
    politicians, 137
    religions, 138
    of the future, 152
  how they operate, 136
  leadership, 143–147
  nostalgia, 130
  rigidity and downfall, 138
Loeb, Marshall, 128
logic, 205–206
logical/mathematical intelligence, 182–183
Lone Ranger, as myth, 80
Lord of the Flies, 90
Lotus Development Corporation, 68
"lunch test," 220

MADD (Mothers Against Drunk Driving), 70
magazines, 99–100
Magic Johnson, 96–97
Major Dad, 87
Makes Me Wanna Holler, 216
management styles, 175–178
managing your life, 170–172
  management styles, 175–178
  portable skills, 173–174
  sense of humor, 175
  support networks, 172–173
Mandela, Nelson, 175
Mary Tyler Moore Show, 98
McCall, Nathan, 216
McCaw, Craig, 58
McLuhan, Marshall, 22, 74
  distortions of reality, 33
  the electronic media, 37
Mead, Margaret, 104
medical schools, 213

memory
  and emotion, 32
  overload, 29–30
  and perspective, 31–33
  what we remember, 31–32
  "menagerie mind," 72–73
  and resilience, 43
mentally ill, in the 1950s, 133
mental maps, patterns, 50
"mental vision," insight, 40
Menozzi, Paola, 215
Micro Dexterity Systems, 59
Microsoft
  management, 177–178
  visualization, 48
  Windows 95, 54
"middle brain," 179–180
mind
  a closed mind, 28
  entrepreneurial, 68–70
  and insight, 40
  interest in, 54–55
  menagerie, 43, 72–73
  mind gyms, 164
  qualities of, 185
  smart work, 19–21
mindless conformity, 198–199
miniaturization, 53–54
minorities. *See also* diversity
  the next minority, 224–227
Mobil Oil, 177–178
Moller, Paul, 56
Monet, 32
money, management, 168–169
Moral Animal, The, 99
Moris, Alene, 170
Morrison, Ian, 201, 204
Morrow, Lance, 131
Morton Thiokol, Inc., 148–149
Mothers Against Drunk Driving (MADD), 70
Mozart, 183
multicultural workforce, 211–214
multiple agendas, 69

multitasking, 162–163
Mundt, Carl, 209
musical/rhythmic intelligence, 183
myths and symbols, 74–77
    the arts, 95–96
    and business, 79–83
    change, 83–86, 89–103
        advertising, 97
        anomalies, 100
        the arts, 95–96
        best-sellers, 98–99
        children's books, 99
        children's myths, 92–94
        death rattles, 101–103
        magazines, 99–100
        new symbols, 96–97
        opposites, 100
        other countries, 101
        "other" networks, 97–98
        science fiction, 94–95
        sitcom trends, 98
        tension, 100
    conservative force, 76–77
    ethnicity, 214–217
    ethnocentric, 89
    gender, 217–219
    global village, 86–89
    myth switches, 89–91
    power of, 75
    race, 214–217
    what are myths, 74–75

Naisbitt, John, 72
nanotechnology, 54, 159
naps, benefits of, 39
Native American men, 132
Navy, a sealed culture, 82
negotiation skills, 165–166
NET, the, 60–62
networking, 172–173
Neural Gyms, 164
new channels, 69
niches
    magazines, 99–100
    picking, 69

Nike, 141
1950s, the, 131–135
1984, 95
Noble, Daniel, 19
nostalgia
    lodge cultures, 130, 135–138
    the 1950s, 131–135
    why a problem, 128–131

observing energy, 160–161
obsolescence, 71–72
odd combinations, 67
Oliver, Mary, 228
opposites, 100
Oregon Steel, 217
organizational cultures, 142
organizing principles, 171
Orwell, George, 95
outside control, 107
Overworked American, The, 169

Parallel Time: Growing Up in Black and White, 216
Parrot S.A., 30
past, the, 128–131
    corporate cultures, 139–143
    lodge cultures, 135–138
    the 1950s, 131–135
patterns and trends
    evolution of, 56–68
        chaos, 67–68
        elaboration, 63–65
        extension, 56–59, 63
        pattern reversals, 66–67
        recycling, 66
        strange attraction, 67
    four basic trends, 53–55
    skills, 70–73
    timing, 52
pendulum swing, change, 123
peripheral males, 216
personal history, 41–42
personal relationships
    balance, 170–172

support networks, 172–173
work hours, 169–170
perspective
distortions of, 33–38
age, 35
class, 36–37
electronic media, 37–38
gender, 35–36
self-righteousness, 34–35
and experience, 28
how it is shaped, 28
importance of, 28
losing, 28–29
and memory, 31–33
skills, 38–49
ability to empathize, 47–48
ability to relax, 39
culture and history, 42–43
insight and intuition, 40–41
insulate hot buttons, 46–47
personal history, 41–42
and the repressed, 44–45
resilience, 43–44
sense of humor, 40
sources of information, 44
tolerance for chaos, 45
visualizations, 48–49
Peters, Tom, 121
Philip Morris, and symbols, 139
photonics, 158–159
physical size, 102
physicians, lodges, 136–137
Piazza, Alberta, 215
Picasso, 183
"plateauing," 166
PMI exercise, 187
polarity thinking, 198
politicians, lodges, 137
portfolio professionals, 173–
174
Potential Rating Index by ZIP
Market (PRIZM), 65
Pound, Ezra, 95
practical intelligence, 184
predicting change, 56–59
prisoners, 100

PRIZM (Potential Rating Index
by ZIP Market), 65
problems
knowing, 193
solving, 185
productivity and myths, 75
Proust, Marcel, 27
Pryor, Richard, 40

questions
flow analysis, 193
recognizing trends, 72

race, 214–217
racial categories, 214–215
radical thinking, 70
Rage of a Privileged Class, 216
reality
class systems, 36–37
culture's history, 42
distortions of, 33
and hot buttons, 46–47
rebuilding, 150–151
recovery, 147–152
recycling, 66
redefinition, 222–224
red-hat thinker, 191
relationships
balance, 170–172
networks, 172–173
self, 171
with time, 154–155
work hours, 169–170
relaxation, 39
religions, lodges, 138
Renier, Jim, 148
repression, 44–45
resilience, 43–44
response time, 104–105
reversals in patterns, 66–67
reverse discrimination, 223
reviews, 168
Road Less Traveled, The, 99
Robinson, Jackie, 212
Rockwell, Norman, 95, 128
Roddick, Anita, 205

Rogers, Will, 182
"roll with the punches," 38–49
Roseanne, 98
Rotstein, Ronald, 54

SAT (Scholastic Assessment
    Test), 180–181
satisfaction, 145
Saudi Arabia, 101
scenarios, 201–202
Scharansky, Anatoly, 175
Scholastic Assessment Test
    (SAT), 180–181
schools
    academics as lodges, 137–
        138
    continuing education, 164–
        165
    managing money, 168–169
    "reduced sport schools," 90
Schor, Juliet, 169
science fiction, 94–95
security
    creating, 160
    insecurity, 155–156
    what is it, 153–154
    at work, 156–160
"seeing the window," 114–
    115
self-righteousness, 34–35
Seligman, Martin, 195
Senge, Peter, 41, 53
    and repression, 44
sense of humor, 40, 175
serendipity, 69
sex
    double standards, 133
    sex roles, 217–219
    techno-sex, 62
Shamier, Jacob, 14
sharing, 118
short-term memory, 30
simplistic thinking, 198–199
Simpson, Alan, 84
Simpson, O.J., 33, 46, 216

Simpson Timber, 29
single motherhood, 133
sitcom trends, 98
Six Degrees of Separation, 86
size, 102
skills
    communication, 165–166
    exploring the future, 201–206
        forecasts, 202–204
        scenarios, 201–202
        wild cards, 204–206
    myth shifts, recognizing
        advertising, 97
        anomalies, 100
        the arts, 95–96
        best-sellers, 98–99
        children's books, 99
        children's myths, 92–94
        death rattles, 101–103
        magazines, 99–100
        new symbols, 96–97
        opposites, 100
        other countries, 101
        "other" networks, 97–98
        science fiction, 94–95
        sitcom trends, 98
        tension, 100
    negotiation, 165–166
    pattern/trend recognition, 70
        ask questions, 72
        keep a journal, 72
        language, 70–71
        menagerie mind, 72–73
        new mixes, 71
        obsolescence, 71–72
        tracing, 70
    perspective, 38–49
        ability to empathize, 47–48
        ability to relax, 39
        chaos, tolerance for, 45
        culture's history, 42–43
        information, sources, 44
        insight/intuition, 40–41
        insulate hot buttons, 46–47
        notice the repressed, 44–45

personal history, 41–42
resilience, 43–44
sense of humor, 40
visualization, 48–49
portable skills, 173–174
thinking, 190
  be humble, 193–194
  beyond the usual, 192–193
  consider EQ, 195
  create alternatives, 191–
    192
  De Bono's hats, 190–191
  evaluate your thinking,
    190
  flow analysis, 193
  review experiences, 194–
    195
  what is the problem, 193
smart guns, 62
Snow White, 92
social thinkers, 186
Socratic Dialogue, 166
space colonization, 159
Spector, Arlen, 84
spiritual intelligence, 184
Staples, Brent, 216
Star Trek, 94–95
status, and size, 102
Stetson-Rodriguez, Marian,
    211–212
Stewart, Baron, 147
Stouffer Chemical Company,
    151
strange attractions, 67
structural thinkers, 186
styles of change, 111–123
suicide, in the 1950s, 132
support networks, 172–173
Surefish, 209
surprise changes, 124–126
survival tales, myths, 75
Switch, 47
symbols, 78–79. *See also* myths
    and symbols
  advertising, 97

systemic change, 120–122
system thinking, 188–189

team-building exercises, 192
"technic" skills, 18
technology, 161–162
  the "cyber" age, 17–19
Teenage Mutant Ninja Turtles,
    67, 93
television
  exported, 87
  the 1950s, 132
  "other" channels, 97–98
  sitcom trends, 98
  why it's addictive, 38
tension, 100
  benefits of relaxing, 39
  change as source of, 104
  creative tension, 100
  "seeing the window," 114–
    115
  and sense of humor, 175
thinking
  barriers to, 196
    absolutes, 196
    being too smart, 198
    contentment, 196
    gender, 200
    gut responses, 199–200
    immediate gratification,
      196–197
    mindless conformity,
      198–199
    polarity thinking, 198
    simplistic, 198–199
    wishful thinking, 198–199
  comparative, 69
  De Bono's hats, 190–191
  hypothetical thought, 69
  polarity, 198
  radical, 70
  simplistic, 198–199
  skills, 190–195
  styles, 185–187
    analytical, 186

thinking, styles (*cont.*)
   conceptual, 186
   lateral, 186–187
   social, 186
   structural, 186
   system, 188–189
   wishful, 198–199
Thomas, Clarence, 83–84, 197
Timberland, 220
time
   importance of timing, 52
   relationship with, 154–155
toilet facilities, 90–91
toleration, 222
tracing, 70
trade, 107
Transformation Leader, The, 148
transitions, 126–127
travel, 107
trends. *See* patterns and trends
Turner, Ted, 86, 205
Turner Broadcasting, 89
20,000 Leagues Under the Sea, 95

understanding who we are,
   22–23

vaporware, 48
vegetables, 110
verbal/linguistic intelligence,
   182
Verne, Jules, 95
"victims," 154
visceral hits, 46
visionaries, 14–15, 35
visualization, 48–49
visual/spatial intelligence, 183

Wal-Mart, 204
Walton, Sam, 43–44

"water logic," 206
Waterman, Robert H., 121
W.A.Y. (Work Appreciation for
   Youth), 165
Way We Were, The, 132
"what-ifs," 204–205
white-hat thinker, 191
wild cards, 204–205
Williams, William Carlos, 179
wishful thinking, 198–199
women
   all-male schools, 89–90
   in foreign countries, 101
   gender myths, 217–218
   in health care, 36
   in the 1950s, 132
   in sitcoms, 98
   toilet facilities, 90–91
   women as liars myth, 83–84
work
   computer technology, 19
   hours worked, 169–170
   smart work, 19–21
   work ethic, 164–165
Work Appreciation for Youth
   (W.A.Y.), 165
workforce
   composition of, as symbol,
      82
   levels of satisfaction, 145
   multicultural, 211–214
   new class system, 19–20
   portable skills, 173–174

xenophobia, 221

yellow-hat thinker, 191

"zero tolerance," 226
zoos, in the 1950s, 133

About the Author

J ENNIFER JAMES IS AN urban cultural anthropologist. She was an academic researcher and lecturer for twenty years. For the last twelve years of her academic career, she was a professor at the University of Washington Medical School. She now lectures throughout the world to corporations and organizations interested in the process of change and new thinking skills, and writes a weekly column for the features section of the *Seattle Times*. She lives near Seattle and is the author of six previous books.

To Contact the Author

To contact Jennifer James for lectures or correspondence:

> Jennifer James, Inc.
> P.O. Box 337
> Seahurst, WA 98062
> Fax: (206) 243-5543
> E-mail: jjanthro@msn.com

Previous books include:

Life Is a Game of Choice, Bronwen Press
Defending Yourself Against Criticism, Newmarket Press
Success Is the Quality of Your Journey, Newmarket Press
Windows, Newmarket Press
Women and the Blues, HarperCollins
Visions from the Heart, Newmarket Press

Enterprise Media, Inc., is currently the authorized distributor of Jennifer James video and audio tapes and CD-ROM.

For a brochure or to order, contact:

> Enterprise Media, Inc.
> 91 Harvey Street
> Cambridge, MA 02140
> Phone: 800-423-6021 (toll-free)
>   617-354-0017
> E-mail: ENTMEDIA@aol.com